Financial Management of the Company Using Change Drivers

Layout & Cover: Books on Demand
Publisher: BoD – Books on Demand, Helsinki, Finland
Manufacturer:Libri Plureos GmbH, Hamburg, Germany
ISBN: 9789528026822

Financial Management of the Company Using Change Drivers

TABLE OF CONTENTS

INTRODUCTION

Here's how it happened again. Having previously written three books I decided that I would not write any more. But having received very positive feedback from clients and my experience with recent client projects, I decided to revisit my previous decision and to write this fourth book after all.

My first book, entitled "KOKO YRITYKSEN KAPASITEETTI TE-HOKÄYTTÖÖN" (= MAKING THE MOST OF YOUR COMPANY'S CAPACITY), was published in August 2022. My second book, entitled "YRITYKSEN VOIMAVARAT HYÖTYKÄYTTÖÖN – YHTEISVOIMIN" (= MAKING THE MOST OF YOUR COMPANY'S RESOURCES – WORKING TOGETHER), was published in February 2023. My third book, "RESURSSIEN TULOKSILLA YRITYKSEN TAVOITETULOKSEEN" (= USING RESOURCES TO ACHIEVE THE COMPANY'S TARGET RESULTS) was published in September 2023. The publisher of all these books is BoD – Books on Demand, Helsinki, Finland, and they are produced by BoD – Books on Demand, Norderstedt, Germany. Without Nadja Melender, BoD's author and publishing consultant, who I met at the BoD stand at the Helsinki Book Fair on 30.10.2021, I would not have written these books. Nadja has acted as BoD's contact person for all matters related to all aspects of my books, including contracts, writing, proofreading, copyediting, editing, cover design, folding, printing and online marketing. All aspects of cooperation with Nadja and BoD have been excellent. A big thank you for all this to both of you and especially to Nadja. They have succeeded with all their efforts in proving that my myth about the laboriousness and inconvenience of writing and publishing a book was unfounded.

To achieve the writing of these four books, the most important motivator has been my beloved wife Seija Manninen. Without Seija's encouragement and support and time away from our time together, I would never have been able to write these four books. A very big thank you to Seija for all this.

A key motivator for the content of this fourth book has been the feedback from readers of my previous three books, which has been very positive and encouraging. In particular, I have been asked me to write my fourth book on the subject of financial management of the firm using change drivers, which is the core of the change management methodology I have developed. In this fourth book in particular, I have focused on the fundamentals, principles and implementation of financial management of the company based on my practical experience in companies. All four of my books complement each other. In my first three books I reveal THE CHANGE DRIVER, the practical application of the change management method and give details of the practical principles of change management.

The contents of all four books are based on my best experiences of change management as a person in charge in companies with a view to achieving goals. In these companies change management has included identifying the necessary change opportunities, selecting the best change opportunities and planning and implementing the changes in practice. In the course of my career, I have addressed these needs by developing several new methods of calculation, applications of target management and new methods of budgeting, based on which the necessary changes can be planned and implemented. For making this possible, a big thank you is due to entrepreneurs, financiers, consultants and other key people in companies. By key people, I mean all key people in companies, from employees to managers, who have been involved in developing business with me in companies and at the same time sought to give concrete evidence of their ability to deliver results as a reference for their own careers. These people have given of themselves in companies many times more than would have been expected of them. They have been motivated by an insatiable passion for learning new skills and put them into practice.

All of these have enabled me to draw on my career experience to write these four books.

My career will continue in the company I founded in October 2022, Muutosdraiveri Oy.

My reflection on this introduction is:

"Happiness does not come from waiting. Happiness comes from your own action in every moment of your life. Everything is possible in life."

AIM OF THE BOOK

The aim of my first book "KOKO YRITYKSEN KAPASITEETTI TEHOKÄYTTÖÖN" (= MAKING THE MOST OF YOUR COMPANY'S CAPACITY) was to explain WHAT start-up entrepreneurs and those who are already entrepreneurs and those who have been in business for a longer period of time need to do in order to achieve their business goals. The aim of my second book "YRITYKSEN VOIMAVARAT HYÖTYKÄYTTÖÖN – YHTEISVOIMIN" (= MAKING THE MOST OF YOUR COMPANY'S RESOURCES – WORKING TOGETHER) was to tell in BRIEF WHAT entrepreneurs already in business need to do, so that their business can achieve its goals on an ongoing basis. My third book "RESURSSIEN TULOKSILLA YRITYKSEN TAVOITETULOKSEEN" (= USING RESOURCES TO ACHIEVE THE COMPANY'S TARGET RESULTS) aimed to give a general overview of what entrepreneurs need to do to get ahead, WHAT existing entrepreneurs need to do to enable their business to achieve its goals on an ongoing basis. The aim of this fourth book "FINANCIAL MANAGEMENT OF THE COMPANY USING CHANGE DRIVERS" is to explain HOW businesses can use electronic information systems to achieve their financial and business goals on a continuous basis. I encourage all entrepreneurs to read this book, so that they have the courage to start growing their business in a controlled way. Too often start-ups wrongly think that recruiting new people into the business is too expensive a way to grow the business. Too often start-ups also get it wrong that it is better to avoid risk in the business and therefore not to recruit. Growing a business by recruiting new people is neither expensive nor risky when it is done correctly, and when it is done with the principles in my four books. This fourth book gives the entrepreneur information on how to achieve his or her financial objectives by continuously using electronic information systems. All four of my books complement each other. How to use the tools I've set out in these books on a company-by-company basis, depends, of course, on the company, its business and its situation. Each company is unique, and therefore the methods I have presented in my books should be applied on a company-by-company basis. When a reader of my books has found concrete ways to improve the performance of his or her company, my books will have achieved their objective.

If a company starts to look for ways to achieve its performance targets solely through external accounting and external performance figures, this information is too superficial. External accounting produces figures that are the result of the activities of the company and the changes made to it within the company. External accounting produces the figures required by law and the financial reports for the company's external stakeholders, including tax and other authorities. If the results of the external accounting of the company are used to design change measures to achieve the company's objectives, it is not possible to change root causes of the profit figures when they are not known. So more in-depth figures on the real root causes of why the company is not achieving its objectives are needed, and in addition to that, in-depth information on what concrete changes in behaviour will best enable the company to achieve its objectives. Internal management accounting is an attempt to provide the information needed to answer these questions, but no company's internal accounting that I have yet seen has been able to provide sufficiently in-depth answers to these questions. As the solution to these problems, I have presented in these three books a method of change management that I have developed and used, called the CHANGE DRIVER. In this book, I focus in particular on how the change management system that enables the financial management of a company using the CHANGE DRIVERS must be created. The using and implementation of CHANGE DRIVERS must be planned on a company-by-company basis, as no two companies are exactly alike. Each company's situation and business owners are unique. All this requires that companies have modern electronic information systems with the right kind of features and that these electronic information systems are used in the way intended.

The main problem in companies is that, based on the company's budgeted targets, they do not know how to set personal targets for each employee in the company. When companies do not know how to do this, the role of the employees in achieving the company's objectives cannot be monitored and understood. When this is the case, it is quite certain that the full capacity of the company is not being used to its full potential.

Once the root causes of the deviations between the actual and target figures of the company are known, they can be used to define target figures for each category and involve them in the development of the company's business in a concrete way. When you add to this the need for change in the company, the right measures to implement the business change and their drivers of change and the impact on results, the company will know how it can achieve its objectives on an ongoing basis. The aim of this book will have been achieved.

This book gives the entrepreneur the basis for knowing HOW he should create the conditions for financial management in his company so that the company's objectives can be realised on an ongoing basis. In this book I have given as much detail as possible on how this must work so that the company can continuously achieve its objectives by using electronic information systems and change drivers in the right way. However, as each company and its situation is individual, in this book I have not been able to give a complete picture of all the different aspects of a company's detailed solutions to all the problems faced by all companies. In all four books, the tools I have presented need to be applied on a company-by-company basis. If this is too much of a challenge for the entrepreneur, then I encourage the entrepreneur to seek outside help, when the entrepreneur's own resources are not sufficient. I do not think it is a weakness, having the courage to ask for help as early as possible. It is a weakness, and stupid as well, to think you know how to plan the change measures that need to be made in the business to achieve the performance targets, even though you do not have the skills to do so. The worst thing is to procrastinate about seeking outside help. The very heart of the matter in the use of electronic information systems and change drivers relies on the ability to define what, how and in what way the company needs to use electronic information systems and change drivers in order to achieve its economic objectives. The vendor of electronic information systems is not the right person to tell you what features the company needs; this definition must be made either by the company's own expert or by an expert chosen by the company. Unfortunately, entrepreneurs are often heard to say that external help is not worthwhile because it is so expensive. Outside help is expensive when it does not recover the costs it causes to the company in the time frame envisaged. What is costly is when a company is constantly making losses, imagining and believing, without any concrete justification, that its results will improve in the future. Beliefs, fantasies and idle gossip explanations do not automatically remedy the company's situation. The only way to bring about a change in a company's results is to take action in doing the right thing.

If the entrepreneur is not able to apply these tools alone, he or she should seek outside help. When the entrepreneur needs external help, it is worth using the right kind of consultant. In particular, I encourage the entrepreneur to use a consultant who has a good understanding of the company's external accounting knowledge and experience of alternative methods of internal accounting and, in particular, their design and practical application in various electronic information systems.

To these aims of the book, my own reflection is:

"By identifying the root causes of a company's financial situation and finding the right solutions to the company's change needs using change drivers, you can bring about lasting change to achieve your business objectives on an ongoing basis."

Trends in business economics

According to the statistics of the National Board of Patents and Registration, there were as at 3.1.2024 a total of 688,991 companies in Finland, whereas on 2.1.2020 there were 616,551, i.e. the number of companies has increased from 2.1.2020 to 3.1.2024 by 72,440 companies As at 3.1.2024, the number of limited liability companies was 288,211 and their number had increased from 2.1.2020 by 22,077 companies. As at 3.1.2024, 257,452 companies were sole proprietorships, an increase from 2.1.2020 by 38,796 companies. Between 2020 and 2023, 154,722 new companies were registered, of which 80,178 were limited companies and 67,243 were sole traders. Between 2020 and 2024, 227,162 companies were deleted from the Commercial Register, of which 58,101 were limited liability companies and 67,243 were sole traders. In other words, there have been a lot of changes in the total number of companies operating in Finland and in the number of different types of companies in Finland between 2020 and 2023. The above figures do not include the number of light entrepreneurs who do not have their own business ID but who are nevertheless active as self-employed persons who invoice their services through invoicing companies, as these numbers of light entrepreneurs are not included in the statistics. Also the number of light entrepreneurs without a business ID has been growing strongly in recent years and will continue to do so.

In Finland, the average size of companies, measured as the number of persons employed by a company is 3 to 4 persons, depending on the method of calculation. This figure has not increased in recent years, but has fallen to this level in recent years in private companies. I think this shows that business growth in Finland is not being adequately achieved through economic management of companies.

The number of self-employed workers has decreased since the beginning of 2015 (94,000 in 2015 to 78,000 in 2023), a reduction of around 16,000. The number of employer firms has fallen from

94,000 in 2015 to 78,000 in 2023. These figures do not include the number of primary production enterprises. In my view, this shows that that there is a lack of economic management skills in Finland as the business cycle changes. I do not think that the change in the business cycle is the reason for this development. Companies can be managed financially in this way, to make sufficient profits in a constantly changing business cycle. This requires that businesses are managed financially in the right way. This book contains solutions on how to manage company finances in the right way.

My summary of the above is that the average size of companies and the number of employer companies must be increased in Finland. When this is achieved in Finland, then Finland will have a sufficient number of sufficiently large companies capable of producing products and services for international markets. If this does not happen, there is a danger that Finland will become a country of small companies and subsidiaries of international companies. For this reason, Finland must remove the obstacles to the growth of the average size of companies and the number of employer companies, and invest in the financial management of companies.

Background on the economic challenges facing businesses

Shortcomings in financial monitoring

During my career, I have helped more than 330 companies to make their business work in line with their objectives, either by leading them or by helping them to identify their business change needs, plan for change and implement change. In all of these companies, the fundamental problem has been a lack of financial monitoring. In practice, this has meant that the necessary monitoring for the financial management of these companies has not been available. More than 90% of these companies had no financial statements, including profit and loss accounts and balance sheets, available for the previous financial year. The figures in the monthly profit and loss accounts could not be relied on because they were recorded on a cash basis. Accrual accounting is an accounting method in which income and expenditure are recognised when the cash flow is realised. In other words, revenues are recognised when they are received and expenses are recognised when they are paid. In these companies, only in the financial statements have the company's income and expenses been accrued in the accounts so that they were allocated to the correct accounting periods on an accrual basis. This was not done on a monthly basis to avoid the costs involved. In the worst cases, even though the company's accounts had been audited by an auditor, the allocation of income and expenditure to the correct accounting period had not been carried out in the financial statements. In these companies, only by following the cumulative quarterly profit and loss accounts could an idea be formed of what the company was producing. Typically, in these companies, budgets were not prepared, cash flow statements were not available and either cash flow forecasts were not prepared or their contents were not reliable.

In the companies I have mentioned above, it has been important, on the basis of the premises I have described, to familiarise oneself with the figures and activities of the companies on a practical level by meeting and putting questions to the people in the companies. This has enabled me to find change agents in these companies, i.e. people with the potential to design and implement the changes I have identified and realise the objectives I have set for them. In order to prevent these companies from running into financial and profitability problems in the future, and to ensure that they continue to achieve the financial objectives that I have set for them, I have had to start by laying the foundations for the financial management of these companies step by step. The starting point for each of these companies was different. The speed with which the financial management foundation could be built in these companies depended on the skills, attitude, willingness and desire of the company's staff to be involved in the necessary change. How far we have progressed with change in these companies during the time I have been designing, implementing, supporting and encouraging these changes has depended on the time available. However, all of the lessons I have shared in this book and in the three books I have written previously, I have been able to try out in these companies, some more and some less.

ACHIEVING THE OBJECTIVES

For example, if there are 50 people working in a company and one person knows the company's financial targets and they have not been communicated to everyone in the company, it is not reasonable to expect that all people will be able to work in the company in such a way that the company's targets are met. Even if the company's management communicates the company's objectives to all the people working in the company, this does not make the situation any easier. When a person is invited to a meeting to hear from the CEO about the company's objectives, typically their thoughts are: Well, it's nice to know the company's objectives by taking a moment away from work, I wonder how we're going to achieve the objectives the CEO told us about, hopefully my employment with the company will continue after all, the CEO seemed really nervous when he told us about the company's objectives, so I guess the company is in a challenging situation. All these thoughts are based on uncertainty, insecurity, worry, fear and the images of the CEO's behaviour in the minds of those invited to the meeting. The question arises: did it happen that, after the CEO told the meeting about the company's objectives, the situation in the company deteriorated in terms of the achievement of the company's objectives? In other words: Did the probability that the company will not achieve its objectives increase when negative thoughts and feelings were evoked in people's minds about the event?

In all simplicity, the steps to achieve the objectives are as follows:

1. Knowing the objectives

2. Doing the work

3. Monitoring the results of the work

4. Getting feedback

Here is an example of company X. From the employee's point of view, the company worked in such a way that the first employee told the subordinate about the work and the steps involved, and the subordinate did the work. How the employee was to do the work in the company depended on his own judgement, i.e. his own perception of how to do the work. When I looked at the way work was done in the company at the following organisational levels, i.e. how the subordinate's superior and his 'superior had worked, their situation in the company was no different. The foreman had recruited the employee's foreman to manage production in the company. What and how he was to do his job depended on his own judgement. The production managed by the front man received orders and the front man tried to fulfil them by managing the production. The company's activities were guided and directed by the orders received, the details of the orders and the perceptions of those involved in carrying out the order as to how they were to do the work associated with the order. How the objective of each order received affected the company's performance, and how the execution of the order affected the company's performance were not known, because the company did not define the objective of each order in the quotation invoice for the order received. The company also lacked order-by-order profitability monitoring. In other words, the company lacked a definition of the objective of the order on the company's performance, i.e. a definition of the impact of the order on the company's performance. In addition, the company did not compare the actual performance of the order with the order's target performance, nor did it compare the actual performance of the order with the order's target impact on the company's performance. In the light of the above, the company's strategy was to execute orders received from customers according to their content, and the company's performance was driven by the content of the orders received and the work done to execute them according to the perceptions of the people who placed them. The harsh truth was that the company's performance was the result of events and not of goal-driven financial management. The owner of the company had set performance targets for the company and, on the basis of these targets, the board of directors had drawn up a strategy for the company and performance targets for the company's results for the next three years.

The company's operational management had not drawn up a business plan or a budget for each financial year on the basis of these data. The strategy for the company, as drawn up by the board of directors, did not correspond at all to my understanding of the real strategy of the company. When I asked the management how the company was managed, the answer was that it was managed on the basis of objectives. When I went on to ask the management of the company how this was done in practice, the answer was that the objectives were to be achieved. My comment on the answers I received is: It is not enough to strive to achieve the company's objectives, they must actually be achieved. This requires not only defining the financial objectives of the company, but also planning, implementation, monitoring, feedback and, if necessary, planning and implementing corrective measures. No wonder that when the company's performance targets were not met, the management's explanations to the board of directors were nothing but guesswork as to why this had happened. When the board of directors asked the company's operational management what they intended to do to correct the company's actual and target performance shortfalls, the answers from the operational management were empty explanations and promises, i.e. verbal acrobatics without concrete action. This had been the company's operational management's way of surviving from one board meeting to the next. When I had carried out a situation analysis of this company, formulated a plan to achieve the performance targets set by the company's board of directors and had presented them to the company's board of directors, the board of directors accepted them. As a result, the CEO of the company was allowed to leave the company and I was contracted to go out and implement the financial management change that I had presented to the company.

PROFITABILITY PROBLEMS

According to Suomen Asiakastieto Oy, there are around 140,000 loss-making companies in Finland every year. My own estimate is that they have on average 3 employees and an average annual turnover of €220,000. The pre-tax operating result of loss-making companies is on average -7% of their turnover, i.e. -€15,400 per year, whereas the pre-tax operating result of these companies should be on average +12% of turnover, i.e. +€26,400 per year. In my opinion, this shows that financial management in Finland is not sufficiently adapted to the changing economic situation. I do not believe that the change in the business cycle is the cause of companies' losses, but that companies must be able to manage themselves financially and make a sufficient profit at all times, even if the business cycle changes. On the basis of the above calculation, the Finnish state loses EUR 140,000 x 41,800 x EUR 0.20 per year in corporation tax revenue from loss-making companies, or EUR 1,170 million per year in corporation tax revenue at the current rate of 20%. On this basis, I believe that the Finnish state should invest, say, EUR 170 million a year in improving the financial management of companies in order to prevent unnecessary losses and improve profits. This would give the Finnish state an extra EUR 1,000 million a year in corporation tax revenue, which it could use to pay off the excessive public debt.

In addition to the number of loss-making companies, another problem related to business profitability is that too many companies in Finland fail to meet their annual profit targets. Having examined this issue with the help of the available statistics, I have come to the following conclusions. There are about 60,000 employer companies in Finland with an average annual turnover of €660,000 and, based on my estimates, an average pre-tax realised operating result that is 5% below the target result set by the owners of these companies. The Finnish state loses corporate tax revenue from these companies to the amount of €0.05 x 660,000 x €0.20 per company per year, or €6,600 per company per year. On this basis, the Finnish state loses €6,600 x 60,000 per year in corporate tax revenue from companies that fail to meet their targets, or €396 million per year. In addition, after corporation tax, these companies will lose €0,05 x 660,000 x 60,'000 x 0.80 per year, or €1,548 million per year.

On the basis of the above figures, I encourage not only the Finnish state but also business owners and management to invest in the financial management of businesses, so that the loss of corporation tax revenue for the Finnish state and the loss of profit for businesses, as I have outlined above, can be translated into corporation tax revenue for the Finnish state and profit for businesses.

Unnecessary bankruptcies

In 2023, a record 3,300 companies filed for bankruptcy. Based on my experience, I estimate that 1,000 of these bankruptcies were unnecessary. The average turnover of these companies was estimated at around €500,000. These companies had an average of 7 employees per company. Because of these 1,000 unnecessary bankruptcies, the Finnish state lost a lot of income from corporation tax and personal income tax for the employees. It is estimated that in 2023 the Finnish state paid out around €33 million in wage guarantee costs, of which the unnecessary bankruptcies accounted for around €10 million. In my opinion, the reason for the unnecessary bankruptcies is that in Finland, in situations of business change, companies are not managed financially and unnecessary bankruptcies avoided. On this basis, it would be worthwhile for the Finnish government to invest in developing the financial management of companies, because the Finnish government has the potential to reap excellent tax benefits from this investment.

Financial Problems of Companies

Financial Problems in Sole Proprietorships

In the case of sole proprietorships, the financial problems are due to the fact that the plans for starting the business have already been poorly made, the plans have been poorly implemented and the monitoring of the business has been poorly done, i.e. the sole proprietor is not in a position to make a profit.

Even if the sole proprietor runs the business alone, it is worth considering what the conditions are for the financial management of the business. It all starts with the fact that a sole proprietor must have access to advice, guidance, help with the necessary calculations, the introduction of financial monitoring and interpretation of the figures for each individual company from professionals with practical experience. It is not enough to ask a start-up sole proprietor to draw up a business plan, a financial statement, a profitability statement, an income statement and a sales statement. They only tell the budding sole trader what to do, but not how to do it. When a sole trader is starting up a business in a completely new situation, one in which he or she may have no previous experience, the budding sole trader will not be able to cope with making these plans and calculations on his or her own. What is essential in drawing up a business plan, financial statement, profitability statement, income plan and sales plan is that the entrepreneur is told and understands where and how to calculate the figures for these plans, and how the starting self-employed person must act in a concrete way to make these figures come true. In addition, the new sole proprietor must be told in a concrete and practical way what opportunities he has to change his own activities and how the implementation of these changes will affect the results of his business, i.e. what the drivers of change are for the business of the sole proprietor.

For the financial management of their business, a sole trader needs a business plan, a financial statement, a profitability statement, an income plan and a sales statement, as well as a real-time cash flow statement and a cash flow forecast. In my opinion, the most important thing for a sole proprietor is to understand what the earnings logic of his business is and how he can influence the development of this through changes in his own activities, i.e. through change drivers. The core of the earnings logic of a business is the profit margin, net of VAT, which includes all the business's costs other than fixed costs, financial charges, repayments on business loans and interest on loans. These costs must be paid on time, and only once the sole proprietor has been able to meet these obligations does he have the opportunity to draw either a salary, holiday pay and related employer's perquisites or a dividend from his business. When the company generates a sufficiently high profit margin, net of VAT, it is the company's "cash-machine", enabling it to achieve its target profit figures.

My warning to the sole trader is: Don't run your business on the basis of its cash flow! This warning applies in particular to VAT-registered businesses. My justification for this warning is that I have seen too many sole traders do this and the result has been that these businesses have both financial problems and payment difficulties.

This warning has two implications:

1. Firstly, the VAT component
    The first point is that VAT on business income and payments is not the entrepreneur's money, it is the taxman's money. In the company's cash resources, this is cash flow belonging to the taxman and therefore must not be used to pay any other payments than VAT to the taxman. If this is not the case, the company may run into payment difficulties when VAT is due if there is no money in the company's cash

resources to pay VAT to the taxman. All too often I have seen these situations in companies that are not profitable.

2. Another important issue is the periodic payment obligations of the company.
This means that certain payments, such as loan repayments or certain insurance premiums, only have to be paid a few times a year. For these payments, the company's treasury must accumulate and set aside cash reserves at all times, which the company may not use to make other company payments. These funds belong to the parties invoicing the periodic payments. For this reason, the company must also keep this money and the VAT payable to the tax authorities separate, so that when the periodic invoices are due, the company's treasury has cash reserves to pay these invoices.

The most important reason for the financial problems of the self-employed is that they do not know how to use their working time in the company properly. All kinds of busy activity, external factors and the momentary thoughts of the self-employed person drive his daily work. Once the business plans of the sole proprietor have been made, he must then plan how he should work in practice in order to achieve the performance targets he has set for his business. Unfortunately, this plan is almost always left undone by sole proprietors. The time management plan of a sole proprietor must answer the following questions:

1. What are the daily working time objectives for the business of the company that the self-employed person must achieve on a daily basis with his/her own working time?

2. How much working time is available to the sole proprietor on a daily basis?

3. How is the daily working time of the sole proprietor to be divided into the following parts:

    3.1 How much of the daily working time does the sole

proprietor aim to use that directly contributes to the company's performance?

3.2 How many hours of the sole proprietor's daily working time do you aim to spend on work that does not directly affect the company's results?

4. How should a sole proprietor spend the hours of his/ her daily working time that directly affect the company's performance?

Once a sole trader has made a daily working time plan, the next step is to stop at the end of each working day to reflect on how he or she has achieved the objectives of the plan. In my experience, it is always the case that the sole proprietor's working time plan and its objectives are not achieved, and the sole proprietor has spent most of his working time on work that has no direct impact on the company's results. As a result of this daily stagnation, the self-employed person must answer the following question: How will I change my own activities tomorrow so that my time-use plan and its objectives are achieved? By continuing this approach on a daily basis, the financial objectives of the business will begin to be achieved.

With a real-time cash flow statement and cash flow forecast, which take into account the VAT and periodic payment obligations described above, the cash flow statement and cash flow forecast are excellent tools for the entrepreneur to develop the solvency and profitability of the business.

Both sole traders and non-entrepreneurs should use the services of accountancy firms with sufficiently sophisticated electronic information systems and real experience and understanding of their clients' practical business. These accountancy firms will then be able to help their clients to develop their business and will not be mere record keepers of their clients' income and expenditure for the purposes of submitting statutory accounts to the tax authorities.

FINANCIAL PROBLEMS IN EMPLOYER COMPANIES

In an employer-owned business, as in any other business, financial problems are caused either by poor profitability or poor solvency. When the profitability of a company is poor, this is usually the reason for its poor solvency. In very exceptional cases, the solvency of a firm may be poor even if it is profitable. In most cases, this is due either to very large advance payments made by the company or to advance payments that the company has had to make much earlier than the revenue it has received for these expenses.

When I think about the remedies for businesses and problems, I always come up with the following engineering-like train of thought on the subject. A company's sales margin is like the company's "money machine', driven by the company's resources. The speed and capacity with which the engine turns the company's "money machine" depends on the speed and capacity with which the company's resources use their resources to turn the company's "money machine". The "money machine' represents the business activities that are in line with the company's strategy. When a firm is in financial difficulty, the amount of revenue the firm earns from the use of the "money machine' in relation to the direct costs to the firm of running the "money machine" is too small to cover all the firm's indirect costs, fixed costs, depreciation, financial charges and the profit target set by the firm's owner. This means that there is one or more of the following possible problems in the use of the "cash machine" by the company:

1. Either the "money machine" produces banknotes that are too small, i.e. the value of one banknote printed by the company is too small in relation to the direct costs incurred by the company in printing one banknote.

2. Or the "money machine" produces banknotes at too slow a rate, i.e. the efficiency of the "money machine" is too low. In practice, this means that the total value of banknotes

printed by the "cash machine" during the period under consideration is too low in relation to the direct costs incurred by the company in using the "cash machine".

3. Or the capacity utilisation rate of the "cash machine" is too low.

If the "money-making machine" of the firm does not have any of the various problems I have outlined above, then one or more of the following costs of the firm are too high: indirect costs of the firm, other costs of the firm, fixed costs, depreciation or financial costs. Among the indirect costs of the firm, I would like to highlight the indirect wage costs of the firm, which may be too high in relation to the firm's sales margin target and/or the sales revenue generated by the firm. Typical financial problems in employer companies are caused either by indirect costs that are too high or by fixed costs that are too high in relation to the sales margin generated by the company.

Perspectives on the financial challenges facing companies

The owner's perspective

From the point of view of the owner of the company, the most important thing is of course whether the company is able to meet all the objectives, financial and otherwise, that the owner has set for the company. If the business is unable to deliver the financially defined objectives, the owner will of course then consider whether it is worthwhile to keep his investment in the business and continue its operations or to exit the business and invest his money elsewhere in more profitable opportunities.

Of the measures of company profitability used by business owners and investors, I believe the most important is the Return On Equity (ROE). It shows the ability of a company to manage the capital invested in the company. The ROE shows how much return on equity has accrued during the financial year. Return on equity is calculated as follows:

Return on equity = 100 x net profit (12 months) / adjusted average equity.

In the case of a financial year other than the normal 12 months, the net result is divided by the length of the financial year and multiplied by 12 before calculating the ratio. The value of equity calculated in this way is the average of the beginning and end of the financial year.

The equity of a company consists of the initial capital contributions of the owners and the profits they leave in the company. The rate of return on equity is largely determined by the return requirements set by the owners. The company must, as a starting point, be able to generate an adequate return not only on equity but also on debt. For this reason, one of the indicators used by owners and investors is the Return On Capital Employed (ROCE), which is calculated as follows:

Return on capital employed =

100 x [net profit + financial charges + taxes (12 months)] / average capital invested

Invested capital = equity + interest-bearing debt.

In the case of a financial year that is different from the normal 12 months, the result of the formula is divided by the length of the financial year and multiplied by 12 before the ratio is calculated.

Invested capital is calculated as the average of the beginning and end of the financial year.

If the equity of the company is negative, the invested capital is always at least equal to the interest-bearing debt.

Return on capital employed is the ratio of the company's performance to the resources needed to generate it, i.e. the capital the company has committed. The minimum return on capital employed is taken to be the interest paid by the company on its borrowed capital. Therefore, a company with a good level of profitability should have a return on capital employed that is well above the interest rate on loans.

The indicative values for the return on capital invested in the company are:

Excellent: more than 15%

Good: 10–15%

Satisfactory: 6–10%

Passable: 3–6%

Poor: less than 3%

Since the riskiness of a company's equity is the highest of all the capital invested in the company, the return on equity must always be higher than the return on a risk-free investment from the market. The risk-free rate of return is usually taken to be the rate of return on government bonds. Since the investment is an equity investment in a risky business, the risk-free return must be increased by a risk premium reflecting the degree of risk. The riskier the company, the higher the risk premium and the higher the return on equity.

The indicative values for the return on equity invested in the company are:

Excellent: more than 20%

Good: 5–20%

Satisfactory: 10–15%

Passable: 5–10%

Poor: less than 5%

The above return on equity and return on capital employed ratios are also suitable indicators for comparisons between companies in different industries.

THE LEGISLATIVE PERSPECTIVE

The legislative perspective in this context refers to the requirements and guidelines laid down by law for the financial management of a company in order to achieve the profitability objectives defined by the company owner.

The Accounting Act (Accounting Act 1336/1997) requires the person charged with keeping accounts to follow good accounting practice (Accounting Act Chapter 1 § 3, Good accounting practice). An accountant must follow good accounting practice. There is no specific definition of good accounting practice in the Accounting Act, but good accounting practice consists of the general laws, rules and regulations governing accounting practice and the general accounting principles that are intended to be followed in practice. This applies both to the recording of transactions in the current accounts and to the preparation of individual and consolidated financial statements. Good accounting practice derives its content from accounting practice and theory. In Finland, the Accounting Standards Board (KILA) plays a key role in guiding practice through its general guidance, opinions and other statements. The Accounting Board, acting in conjunction with the Ministry of Economic Affairs and Employment, issues general instructions, statements and opinions on the application and interpretation of good accounting practice on the basis of the mandate enshrined in the Accounting Act (Chapter 8 § 2 of the Accounting Act), and thus plays a central role in guiding and developing compliance with good accounting practice.

In the following, I have set down some of the main and general accounting principles from the Accounting Act:

Financial statements must give a true and fair view of the results of operations and financial position in accordance with the principle of materiality, taking into account the nature and extent of the activities carried out by the person subject to the accounting obligation (Accounting Act, Chapter 3, Section 2).

An item is material when its omission or misstatement could reasonably be expected to influence the decisions of users taken on the basis of the financial statements. Even if an item is individually immaterial, the assessment of materiality should be made in the context of the whole if there are several similar items (Accounting Act, Chapter 3, Section 2a). This is the materiality principle.

Presumption of continuity of the activity of the accounting entity (Accounting Act Chapter 3 § 3). This is the principle of continuity. Once selected, the accounting periodicity and valuation solutions are followed from one financial statement to the next. The reader of the financial statements must be confident that the differences between two successive sets of financial statements are not due to changes in the way the information is treated but to actual changes in activity. This is the principle of consistency.

Consistency in the application of accounting policies and methods from one financial year to the next (Accounting Act, Chapter 3, Section 3).

Attention to the substance of transactions and not merely to their legal form (Accounting Act, Chapter 3, Section 3). This means that transactions are recorded in the accounts according to their actual content. This is the principle of substance.

Taking account of income and expenses for the accounting period, regardless of the date of payment of the payments due (Accounting Act, Chapter 3, § 3). This is the accrual principle.

Minor entries made on an accrual basis or a cash basis do not need to be adjusted and restated to the accrual basis before the financial statements are prepared, unless their combined effect is material (Accounting Act, Chapter 3, Section 4). This is a clarification of the accrual principle.

If the micro-company is an association or foundation, it may also prepare its accounts on a cash basis, provided that it is not the parent company of a group for which consolidated accounts must be prepared (Accounting Act, Chapter 3, Section 4). This is an exception to the accrual principle.

All companies should keep accounts and in most cases it is compulsory. The obligations to keep accounts and publish financial statements depend on the size and form of the company. In my view, it is worth right from the beginning keeping company accounts in such a way that they are kept without any facilitation of the publication of the company accounts. In this way, the company learns from the outset how to prepare its accounts in a correct and sustainable way.

From the point of view of the financial management of the company and the achievement of the company's profitability objectives, I would like to highlight one of the following points from the Accounting Act: "Accounting for income and expenses for the accounting period, regardless of the date of payment of the payments based on them" (Accounting Act, Chapter 3, Section 3). This is the accrual principle. Especially in small and medium-sized companies, only the profit and loss accounts are prepared in such a way that only the financial statements account for the company's income and expenses in the accounts, i.e. they are allocated to each other and to the correct accounting periods. The reason for this practice in these companies is to reduce accounting costs. In these companies, when the operational management of the company asks for monthly profit and loss accounts in order to know what the company's results are, these figures are in reality what they are because of the non-accrual nature of the income and expenditure. These monthly profit and loss account figures do not tell us anything about the real profitability of the company. In these companies, the true profitability of the company is only revealed in the company's financial statements, when profitability figures typically plummet. In addition to the non-accrual nature of income and expenditure, these companies typically do not accrue, for example, holiday pay and periodic expenditure in the monthly profit and loss accounts, making it even more likely that profitability will collapse in the company's financial statements. In these companies, it is advisable to use cumulative profit and loss accounts that include provisions for holiday pay and holiday pay. When the cumulative profit and loss account figures include figures for at least two months, or preferably three or four months, from the beginning of the financial year, the cumulative profit and loss accounts already provide a much more accurate indication of the company's profitability situation. Even this method is not sufficient, in my opinion, and therefore in this book I will describe in more detail the solutions to this problem.

THE COST ACCOUNTING PERSPECTIVE

Traditional cost accounting methods are old-fashioned calculation methods with the following three stages:

1. Cost accounting, which involves determining the total costs of the company for the accounting period, for example purchases, by cost category.

2. Cost centre accounting, where the indirect costs of the company are allocated to cost centres, e.g. inventory to a purchasing cost centre.

3. Activity-based costing, where indirect costs are allocated to outputs, such as products and services, using either allocation or incremental costing to allocate indirect costs.

The weakness of traditional cost accounting methods is that indirect costs are allocated to products and services on a volume basis rather than on the basis of the resources needed to produce them. As a result, traditional cost accounting methods do not allocate indirect costs to products and services correctly according to the principle of causation, especially for low-volume products and services.

The activity-based costing method has been developed to correct errors in traditional costing methods. In activity-based costing, resources and their costs are first allocated to activities and then from activities to objects such as products and services. All accounting methods, like activity-based costing, must be applied on a company-by-company basis. The application of all accounting methods must be continuous and not just a project.

The shortcomings of traditional cost accounting methods have led to the development of traditional Activity-Based Costing (ABC). Traditional activity-based costing requires the use of multiple drivers to allocate costs. As a result, the application of traditional activity-based costing is complex and expensive to both create and maintain. The implementation of traditional activity-based costing in organisations often results in rising costs and illogical employee behaviour. Traditional activity-based costing requires employees to estimate how much time they spend on different activities. The larger and more complex the organisation, the more challenging it is to implement traditional activity-based costing.

As a solution to this problem, Kaplan and Andersson have developed Time-Driven Activity-Based Costing (TDABC). In time-based activity-based costing, there are two cost parameters: the cost per unit of time (€/min) and the time taken to perform the activity. The cost per time unit must include all resource costs, divided by the target time to perform the activity at the planning stage and the actual time of performing the activity at the implementation stage. Companies using time-based activity accounting do not quantify or often fail to quantify unused capacity (Grasso, L. 2005, 14) because they do not monitor the distribution of paid working time between time spent on accounting objects and time not spent on accounting objects by the employee. In practice, time-based activity accounting is a complex and expensive solution to create and develop on a company-by-company basis, so that there is a reason why this monitoring of the distribution of working time has been omitted, although this is a major shortcoming from the point of view of the financial management of the company.

As both traditional activity accounting and time-based activity accounting do not sufficiently link the financial figures of a company to its operations for operational management purposes, a two-dimensional activity accounting model has been developed for activity accounting. In addition to the cost dimension of activity accounting, a process dimension has been developed. The process dimension focuses on the observation of the processes of the company.

The aim is to obtain information on the performance of tasks related to processes and how they affect the performance of activities. In particular, the process dimension seeks to find out what the work done in the company's processes entails and how well this work is performed. The aim is to enable the company to use this information to develop its business. In my opinion, the process dimension in activity-based accounting is a good thing, but the crucial issue in using the process dimension in activity-based accounting is how to implement it simply and effectively enough as part of the overall financial management of a company.

In general, the problem for companies is that their processes have become very complex and multifaceted. When there have been problems in the steps of the business processes, they have been addressed by adding resources and steps to the problem areas, with the result that the business process has become more complex. This approach has not been used to identify and correct the root causes of the problems, but to identify and correct the consequences of the problems. While a company's activity-based costing system is complex and expensive to create and maintain, simply allocating costs makes it even more complex and expensive to create and develop. In my view, the process dimension of activity-based costing is a good thing in itself, because company management needs more information than just cost data for financial management of the company. The main problem with activity-based costing, and with any other method of providing financial information to support operational management of a company, is that it does not meet the need. All information production should focus only on obtaining relevant and sufficiently accurate financial information for the operational management of the company. It is better to be roughly right than exactly wrong.

Everything the company does is about delivering the results it wants with the lowest possible investment. To achieve this goal, cost accounting is only one option in the operational management of a company. Other key opportunities are the characteristics of the products sold by the company, the content of the services sold by the company, the efficiency of the use of resources, the productivity of resources and capacity utilisation. The key question is how to take account of all these possibilities in the operational management of a company in the most cost-effective way.

After observing the problems I have described above, I decided to look for an answer to this question. In response to this question, I have developed the CHANGE DRIVER method of change management, which is based on the financial management of a company using change drivers.

The financial management perspective

There are two important requirements for the financial management of a company, both of which must be taken into account when managing a company financially.

The first requirement for the financial management of a company is that every task carried out in the company must contribute to the results defined by the owner of the company. This requirement means that all the direct and indirect activities of the company must be able to be carried out in accordance with the objectives set for them. When the results of all the work carried out in the company are added together, they constitute the company's actual result. This requirement is easy to understand and to state, but to put it into practice requires experience-based insight. In practice, this means that all the work carried out in a company must have an objective, a plan and a monitoring system to verify that the objective has been achieved. This, in turn, requires that the company have an understanding of how all the work carried out in the company contributes to the achievement of the company's target result. In addition, each task in the company must be carried out competitively, i.e. the requirement is that all the company's work be carried out with the best possible resources and in the best possible way. This requirement is to achieve the objectives defined by the owner of the company by carrying out all the work in the company in a cost-effective and competitive manner.

Another requirement for the financial management of a company is that all investments in the capacity of the company must produce a result defined by the company owner for the total capacity of the company. This requirement is to achieve the objectives defined by the owner of the company for the return on the investments made in the capacity of the company. Unfortunately, this requirement is often overlooked, especially after the investments in capacity have been made, and the focus is on using only the resources of the firm in a cost-effective manner.

All of the above requirements mean that everything you do in a business must be based on working for the profit of the business, either directly or indirectly through work that affects the profit of the business. Even if the work done indirectly affects the company's performance, the work that indirectly affects the company's performance must nevertheless, and especially for that reason, have as tangible an effect as possible on the achievement of the company's performance. If there is no such impact, then all such work in the company is, in my view, fundamentally unnecessary. If this opinion of mine can be proven wrong in a concrete and economic way, then I am prepared to change my opinion in these cases. But not otherwise. It is indeed healthy whenever companies take a sceptical and critical view of all indirect labour and start to question the real and concrete necessity of indirect labour and its importance for the company's results. When companies bring to people's attention in a concrete way the importance of the work done by all people to the company's results, it opens people's eyes, so to speak, to the importance of work in a new way. In my experience, people have not been told about the importance of their work for the company's results and they do not know how to think about it themselves. When people are told how the work they do affects the company's performance and how people can affect the company's performance by changing the way they do their assigned work, the light bulb of understanding always lights up in people's heads and they are eager to improve the way they do their assigned work. So what are the typical reasons why not all people in companies are told about the importance of their work to the company's performance? These reasons are typically that either the company has not wanted to tell people about the financial impact of their work on the company's performance or has not been able to tell them.

In one company, when I asked the HR manager, "Why are these things not communicated to the staff?", he replied: "If you tell people about the importance of their work to the company's bottom line, they will ask for too much pay." I asked the HR manager, "Could staff be paid more than they are now if they can increase the productivity of their work?" The HR manager asked me: "Can you give me an example?". I gave the example of a case where a person has so far been able to do an average of 15 pieces of work per hour, and now he has found a new and acceptable way of doing an average of 20 pieces of work per hour. Having said this, I asked the HR manager: "Is the person entitled to receive the part of his improved productivity in the form of better pay that belongs to him, and the company receives the part of this increase in productivity that belongs to the company?" Having heard this, the HR manager replied to me: "Of course the person is entitled to receive more pay for doing so." When I then asked the HR manager whether he thought it was worthwhile to increase productivity in the company in a way that would benefit both the staff and the company, the HR manager replied: "Of course it is worthwhile to increase productivity in the company in this way." I suggested to the HR manager: "Increase the financial awareness of staff in the company about their possibilities of influencing the productivity of their work and develop a performance bonus scheme as an incentive." The HR manager said, "That's a good idea." At the same time he asked me: "Can I present this idea to the CEO of the company?" I said, "Of course you can." The upshot of all this was that the HR manager presented my proposal as his own idea, which the CEO accepted, and I was given a new mandate to propose a performance bonus scheme for the company's staff. I made a proposal that was accepted and implemented by the company.

I think everyone gained by this change. All's well that ends well. While at the beginning the HR manager was against telling people about the importance of their work to the company's bottom line, he later changed his mind. I think this is a good example of how you can get people to embrace change in a positive and empowered way. Even if you have a negative attitude towards change, it is not worth forcing change on people. It is worth selling the change to the person who is against it so that they can change their attitude to change on their own initiative. This is done by asking the right questions in series, in the right way and in a fearless atmosphere. By answering the questions asked on their own initiative and using their own common sense, they can change their mind and their attitude to change. The aim should not be to assume that answering the questions in the questionnaire will in itself change the respondent's attitude to change. When the respondent is forced to think deeply enough about his or her answers to the right questions, the aim should be that the respondent himself or herself realises the need for change and has a positive attitude towards change in the future. There are many reasons why a person may have a negative attitude to change. For example, a person is negative about change because other people in the company are negative about it, or at least the company's opinion leaders are negative about it. It may be that the person has not even considered or been able to consider how the change will affect their work. In this case, especially changes whose effects are either not communicated or not communicated in the right way cause people to be afraid. If the communication of change is so badly handled, then I think it is no wonder that there is resistance to change, at least until we know what we are resisting. When you conduct interviews, you often find that people's words and actions do not match up. Well, that's the way we humans are sometimes. Some more often than others. But as a consolation, it is good to remember that we humans do not lie with our minds, but we can lie with our thoughts. When you can change your thoughts and be honest with yourself, you can change. Therefore, thoughts and changing them are the key to any change. Ultimately, in any change, only the actions and the results of doing them matter.

From sport I have learned a good principle that also applies to change and change management. In sport, it is not enough to go to competitions and do your best to be successful. I think this is the wrong attitude, although you hear it too often from athletes these days. When a sports journalist asks an athlete, "What is your goal for the upcoming competition?" the athlete replies, "I will go to the competition and do my best." Going into the competition, you have to have a winner's attitude. You don't go to the competition to lose, you go to the competition to win. When an athlete's pre-race performance in a competition is not enough to win, then the athlete's attitude and goal is to surpass themselves in order to win the competition. If the athlete does not have this attitude, then in my opinion it is a fitness sport and not a competitive sport. It is the same thing in business and change management. If people do not have the will to excel when necessary, then they cannot learn and achieve. Without a winner's attitude, progress stops.

INFORMATION SYSTEMS PERSPECTIVE

The needs of companies for the use of electronic information systems, and the characteristics required of information systems, must be defined for each company. Today, there are many good options on the market for electronic financial management systems for start-up entrepreneurs. In my opinion, it is advisable for start-up entrepreneurs to choose an electronic financial management system and an accounting firm for their company as soon as it is established, one which will be able to carry out the accounting and financial statements of the start-up company and help the entrepreneur to create the conditions for the financial management of his company and to manage it accordingly. Especially after the company has become an employer company, the need to use and develop internal accounting becomes a very important prerequisite for the company if it is to achieve its financial objectives on a continuous basis.

Electronic financial management systems typically include the following features:

Accounting

Financial statement

Invoicing

Payment

Payroll

Inventory management and products

Cash flow and profit and loss budgeting, monitoring and forecasting

When a company's business is based on buying and selling products, the financial management system described above enables the entrepreneur to manage his company financially and, with the right financial management system, to obtain reporting that is comprehensive enough for the operational management of the company.

The limitations of a business financial management system come into play very quickly as a business grows, and especially when the business of a business involves more than just buying and selling products. In such cases, the financial management of the company requires other electronic systems in addition to the company's financial management system. Here are a few examples.

When a company's business is based on services, especially the use of invested machinery and vehicles for the core business of providing direct services to customers, the company typically needs an electronic ERP (Enterprise Resource Planning) system in addition to an electronic financial management system. In order to achieve an adequate level of financial management, the company needs an electronic ERP system, typically with the following features:

Quote calculation

Order management

Planning and management of operations, in particular the use of direct resources (people, machines, vehicles)

Procurement

Integration with the company's financial management system

The company's electronic financial management systems are designed to produce financial management reports such as profit and loss accounts, cash flow statements and balance sheets. Electronic financial management systems are typically not designed to produce internal accounting reports for the needs of the company's operational management and therefore have very limited capabilities. Typically, it is the features of eFMS (electronic Financial Management System) where the limits come into play:

1. When profitability reporting is required

    1.1   By product.

    1.2   By project.

    1.3   By customer.

    1.4   By subcontractor.

    1.5   By activity.

    1.6   By resource.

    1.7   By region.

1.8   By business function.

2.   When reports need to include information from other
     electronic systems in the company for both budgeting
     and monitoring purposes. This is particularly relevant for
     variance monitoring, which is related to monitoring the
     efficiency of the company's operations and the capacity
     utilisation of resources.

When the limits of an electronic financial management system
are reached, for example when its capabilities are not sufficient,
the company needs an electronic reporting system (BI) in addition
to the electronic information system for financial management
and ERP. In the past, companies only had access to massive,
cumbersome and expensive reporting systems that allowed
them to "drill down" into their business, which meant that only
large companies were able to use these systems. Fortunately,
there have been very positive changes in the reporting systems
market, which have resulted in the availability of new-technology-
based electronic reporting systems for small and medium-sized
companies. They offer excellent integration possibilities with
other electronic information systems in companies. In addition,
these new types of reporting systems are in most cases easily
customisable to the financial management needs of companies
at a reasonable cost.

In addition to the above, there are also other information
systems for companies on the market, such as CRM (Customer
Relationship Management) systems, but their use and necessity
must be assessed on a company-by-company basis, i.e. how their
use has a concrete and measurable impact on the company's
performance and how quickly the investments made in these
electronic information systems will pay off in terms of enhanced
company performance.

THE SKILLS PERSPECTIVE

The skills perspective in companies

When I look at the need for skills in companies, the starting point is that a company has sufficient skills to make the products it sells and provide the services it sells, given the diversity of its business activities. On the other hand, firms lack the skills needed for financial management. Without this shortage, all firms would be able to achieve their performance targets on a consistent basis. Looking at this issue in more detail from my own experience, the question arises: What are the financial management skills that are most often lacking in companies, which are essential for companies and which prevent companies from achieving their performance targets on a consistent basis? My answer to this question is that companies mostly lack the right pricing skills. Nevertheless, it is worth remembering that each company is unique, and so their skill gaps are also unique.

In the following, I will go through the principles of calculating the selling price of one VAT-exempt product in a company that manufactures its own product. The calculation of the VAT-free selling price of a company's product consists of two parts, which are:

1. Calculating the cost of manufacturing the product.

2. The allocation of the other costs of the company to the product manufactured.

Companies are usually able to calculate, on a product-by-product basis, the cost of the raw materials and parts purchased for the direct manufacture of the product and how much they cost per product manufactured. If these purchases involve storage in the company, the purchase costs must be multiplied by a company-specific purchase price factor, which is often not done. In addition, companies usually know how many man-hours are needed to manufacture a product, who the workers are, what their hourly wages are and how much they cost the company in direct labour costs per product. Since these direct wage costs do not yet represent the total direct wage costs incurred by the firm in producing the product, the direct wage costs must be multiplied by a wage cost factor in product pricing, which covers all employer contributions, holiday pay and holiday pay related to the direct wage costs. Even this is not enough: the direct wage costs must also be multiplied by a factor to cover the other wage costs incurred by the company in producing the product, such as the cost of hours worked, the cost of sick leave and other costs per hour of production. There are too many shortcomings in companies' ability to correctly calculate the above coefficients. Then add to the cost of manufacturing a product the indirect costs of manufacturing the product, e.g. the cost of the labour involved in manufacturing the product. The cost of manufacturing a product is obtained by adding together

1.   The purchase cost of the product multiplied by the purchase price multiplier, if the product is manufactured with storage.

2.   The direct labour costs associated with the manufacture of the product multiplied by their marginal cost multiplier multiplied by the incremental cost multiplier.

3.   Indirect costs associated with the production of the product.

The next step is the most demanding stage of product pricing, which is to determine the other costs of the company to be added to the manufacturing costs of the product, namely:

1.   The share of the other common costs of the company to be allocated to the product.

2.   The share of the firm's fixed costs to be allocated to the product.

3.   The share of the company's depreciation-related imputed costs to be allocated to the product.

4. The share of the company's financial charges allocated to the product.

5. The share of the company's pre-tax profit target set by the board of directors of the company allocated to the product.

When calculating the other costs to be allocated to the product, the following should be taken into account. The product is manufactured for about 10.5 months per year, but these costs are incurred over 12 months per year. For this reason, when calculating the other costs attributable to the product, a factor of $12 / 10.5 = 1.143$ should be used.

When calculating the other costs attributable to the product, these should be calculated on the basis of the cost principle, so that the sales prices calculated for each product are not distorted.

The main errors in the calculation of the VAT-exempt selling prices of products manufactured by a firm are made in the calculation of the other costs attributable to the product.

The selling price of a product net of VAT is the cost of manufacturing the product plus the other costs of the business added to the cost of manufacturing the product.

Perspective of competences in the services needed by companies

When a company needs external expertise for its business, it is typically in one of the following situations:

1. This is a skill that is required for the company's business on a momentary basis and which the company does not normally need to run the company's business, i.e. it is not part of the core skills required for the company's business.

2. Or it is not part of the core competence necessary for the firm's business, but the firm needs to purchase this service

from outside the firm when the firm's own capacity is not sufficient to provide the service to the firm's customers, i.e. it is a momentary need for the firm's supply capacity during peak market demand.

3. The firm purchases the service from outside the firm because the firm is unable to provide the service in question as an in-house service at competitive prices compared with the prices of service providers available outside the firm.

Above, I have outlined typical business-needs-driven situations in which companies buy services from external service providers. These situations involve either a temporary need for services or a specialised expertise, where the decision on the choice of the service provider is based on the purchase price of the service. Much more important than the purchase price of the service, for example in euros per hour, is what the company gets from buying the service. If this issue is considered from the point of view of the financial management of the company, as it should be, then the company must compare the value added that it obtains from the services it buys from external service providers. This benefit is defined in terms of the extent to which the firm is able to improve its performance by purchasing these services from outside the firm. Before a firm purchases services from outside, it must define the content of the service it is purchasing and what it is willing to pay for the service it has defined. The company must be able to tell its supplier the price of the service, either in euros per service or at a fixed price. In this context, I would like to emphasise that, in the context of financial management, the company buys its external services from service providers who are able to provide the best added value for the company and at the same time meet the other objectives defined by the company for the purchase of the service, such as quality criteria and the like.

Solutions to Achieve the Objectives of the Book

Operational analysis

Before undertaking a business analysis of a company, it is worthwhile to get an overall picture of the company's business. The information needed to do this can be obtained by interviewing members of the company. As a result of the interviews, the interviewer must be able to form a good enough overall picture of the company's business to be able to describe the essential interdependencies between the company's activities and operations in a FLOW diagram, a single image of no more than A4 size, and in a way that is easy to read and understand. This is particularly important because the interviewer needs to present the overall picture to the key people in the company to ensure that he has understood things correctly, and that he has been able to include all the essential parts of the company's business. So why does the interviewer need to draw a FLOW diagram of the company's operations? You need to be able to draw a picture, because drawing a picture requires the interviewer to be able to understand the essential parts of the company's business and their interdependencies. My experience of drawing is that drawing the business as a picture in a FLOW diagram requires several iterations until the solution to drawing the picture is realised. Keeping the size of the picture to A4 at most ensures that the picture does not contain too much detail, but is large enough to contain all the essential information. In this context, it is often argued that there are so many different things going on in a company that it is impossible to capture all its activities on a FLOW diagram in an A4 size image at most. That's not the point – you have to be able to focus on the essentials when drawing the picture. The next step is to carry out an analysis of the company's activities.

The change drivers of corporate financial management are based on an analysis of the company's performance. Before a company can implement corporate financial management with change drivers, an analysis of the company's activities is necessary. In particular, the business analysis is a tool for improving the performance of the company, i.e. for making more efficient use of all its resources and capacities, and for laying the foundations for the financial management of the company through change drivers. The business analysis should be carried out at the level of the company's activities by interviewing key people in each of the company's activities. In this context, the functions of the firm are:

1. Marketing

2. Sales

3. Direct production

4. Indirect production

5. Possible internal service to production, e.g. maintenance service

6. Financial management

7. Management

The aim of the interviews is to obtain answers to the following questions from key people in each function:

1. Who is the customer of the function, either outside or inside the company?

2. What is the purpose of the activity?

3. What services does the activity provide to its customer(s)?

4. What are the expectations of the customer/customers for the services provided by each activity?

5. Why do the client/clients want/need to use the services provided by the activity?

6. What is the estimate of the number of different services the activity provides to its client/clients per year?

7. What is the estimate of how much of the activity's resources are needed to provide the services and how much for other activities of the activity?

8. What are the costs of each activity per year?

9. What are the capacities of each activity?

10. What are the objectives of each activity?

11. What are the tasks performed by the services provided by the activity?

12. What ideas for improvement does the key person in the function have for developing the function's activities?

The aim of question 11 is to record the work to be done by function in a list.

Interviewing key people in a company's operations always brings up new and surprising issues. They should be approached with open curiosity and focus on the essentials. The more experience a business operations analysis interviewer has in interviews, the more he or she will usually have the ability to read the interviewee based on the interviewee's behaviour during the interview, his or her attitude to the interview questions, the interviewer's ability to get the interviewee to open up during the interview, and the interviewer's ability to read between the lines of what the interviewee is saying.

When these questions are asked in a company, it is almost always either impossible to answer them or, in any case, the answers given are incomplete. The purpose of asking these questions is to obtain the necessary information on the current state of the company's business and, at the same time, to identify areas for improvement. When these questions are put to key people in the function, they almost always have very good ideas for improving the performance of the function. And when you ask them if they have presented these suggestions to their own managers, the standard answer is yes: "I have not bothered to propose all these ideas to my manager, as I have not received any feedback from my manager on any of my other ideas." In the worst cases, the feedback from the supervisor has been: "Don't worry about these things, just do your job. That's what you get paid for."

While the company typically lives day to day, so to speak, doing the jobs that are needed most at the moment to get through the day, the company has been resourced and told what to do based on the needs of the moment, or in the worst cases, the front-line person has told the recruit to ask the rest of the function for their work needs. In such cases, the company is driven by momentary needs and not run on an economic, change-driver-driven basis. There really is a lot of untapped potential in these companies to improve the company's performance.

Once the interviewer has interviewed the key people in all functions of the company, the next step is to start tracking the results of the services they provide in each function, by function, at the level of the function, as needed. This is because the monitoring data needed for the financial management of a company in change management is not available for companies. The essential elements of these monitoring activities are to monitor, by activity, the following:

1. What are the service outputs and how much does the activity produce during the monitoring period?

2. How many man-hours per service are used to directly

provide the different services of the activity during the monitoring period?

3. How many indirect man-hours per service are used to provide all the services of the activity during the monitoring period?

4. What are the possible causes of the problems encountered by the activity during the monitoring period and what is the estimate of the causes of these problems?

5. What ideas for improving the operation can you think of during the monitoring period?

Conducting interviews with key persons in the company's functions on a function-by-function basis in the field has many advantages over conducting interviews with key persons in the company in the office. Here are some justifications for this approach:

1. When interviews are conducted in the office, the interviewer forms his/her perception of the company's operations based on the interviewee's account.

2. When the interviewer conducts the interviews in the field as much as possible, it is easier for the interviewer to get a true picture of the company's operations when he can use his hearing and sight to form it.

3. By conducting interviews in the field as much as possible, the interviewer has the opportunity to use his or her instincts based on experience to ask additional questions, thus broadening his or her understanding and deepening his or her knowledge of the company's actual operations. At the same time, the interviewer will be able to avoid possible misinformation about the company's activities from a well-informed interviewee.

4. When the interviewer conducts interviews in the field as much as possible, this is an effective way of breaking down any misconceptions about the roles, actions and perceptions of the company's operations. In addition, finding non-value-added work and tasks in the field is possible by using visual observations and asking additional questions of the interviewee if necessary.

5. When you stop to talk ex tempore with other people during key informant interviews in the field, typically they will openly talk about their work and the things that make it difficult for them to do their job. At the same time, getting answers to additional questions from them is always productive.

6. After the interviewer has conducted the interviews in the field, it is certainly worthwhile to complete the interviews by interviewing the front-line staff. This will allow the interviewer to challenge the interviewee's perceptions of the issue, if necessary, based on the results of the key informant interviews in the field, and to ask the interviewee more specific questions about the issue.

As a result of the analysis of the company's activities, the company will have access to the results of the monitoring by activity, which the company will need when it comes to introducing change drivers at the activity level in the financial management of the company. In addition, as a result of the analysis of the company's activities, the company will have access to a list of tasks to be performed in each activity. This list will be used by the company to analyse the work within the activities, the need for it, the methods used to carry it out and the results of the work, if necessary, at a later stage.

In the following, I will describe my interview experiences with companies in relation to change and its management.

The most challenging case in my career was the following one. An entrepreneur started a business on his own. He grew his business and recruited new people into his business as he saw fit. The entrepreneur really had to make all the decisions himself. When the number of employees increased to more than ten, the entrepreneur felt the need to hire the first indirect person as a foreman in his company, but without the decision-making power, which remained with the entrepreneur. As the company continued to grow, the entrepreneur recruited more employees and intermediaries, first for sales and then for production and procurement. However, the entrepreneur continued to operate throughout, with decision-making power remaining with him. In other words, the principle of the company was that the entrepreneur decided and others did the work. When the entrepreneur heard or observed problems in the company, he would always ask indirect persons what the cause of the problem was. When this had been going on in the company for a long time, the indirect persons stopped thinking about the root causes of the problems because they had lost the motivation to find them due to a lack of responsibility. Their attitude was that there was no point in thinking about the challenges and opportunities of the company when they were not in a position to influence them. When the entrepreneur either heard or noticed a problem in the company, he told the indirect persons and asked what the problem was. The typical answer was that the problem was due to a lack of human resources. As a result, the entrepreneur decided to recruit more human resources to the company and the indirect persons did not have to find out the root causes of the problems, i.e. the real concrete causes. A culture of managing the consequences of the problems had emerged in the company. As the company continued in this way for some time and competition in the market became more intense, the level of sales prices fell in relation to rising costs. As a result, the company found itself in financial difficulties, and when the entrepreneur, together with the company's intermediaries, could not find a solution to the situation, I was commissioned by the entrepreneur. My task was to draw up as quickly as possible a proposal for a plan to solve the company's financial problems as quickly as possible. The entrepreneur gave me two months to prepare the proposal.

I started the assignment by looking at the financial figures of the company. For the purpose of my assignment, I only had access to the company's financial statements. I had access to the company's monthly profit and loss figures, but they did not correctly break down income and expenditure, so I could not use them for my assignment. All other monitoring was for individual issues and was not linked to the company's external accounting figures. For example, as projects progressed, the company monitored the number of hours worked per project in relation to those calculated for the project in the tender calculation of the order received. The company did not have a project-by-project profitability monitoring system in place and therefore could not compare, on a project-by-project basis, how well the profitability of the project was achieved against the profitability targets set in the order quotation.

When I could not find out the causes of the company's financial problems from its financial figures, I set out to learn more about the company's operations and make some visual observations. At the same time, I selected the interviewees purely on the basis of what I saw, i.e. I looked for people who were interested in the company's activities. Sometimes I interviewed people working directly and sometimes I interviewed people working indirectly. My intention was simply to find problems and opportunities for improvement in the company's activities and to ask people for ideas for improvement.

Right from the start, I found out that the company hadn't raised prices for contract customers for years, so we made a phased decision to raise prices. At the same time, when I found out about a major cost problem, the entrepreneur wanted me to speed up the assignment I had received so that my proposal to solve the company's financial problems would be ready within three weeks. I promised to do this and told the entrepreneur that since the company did not have the financial management conditions in place with the change drivers, I would have to base my proposal solely on the company's financial statements and my interviews. At the same time, I told the entrepreneur that by implementing my proposal, the company would be able to get out of its financial problems temporarily, but not permanently. When I presented my proposal to the entrepreneur within three weeks, the entrepreneur asked me to help them, if necessary, to implement the changes to my proposal, and this was agreed. Once my solution was in place, the entrepreneur asked me to come up with a proposal on how the company could get out of its financial problems permanently. I suggested to the entrepreneur that the solution was to create a culture, a way of working, in which the financial management of the company would be carried out with change drivers. The entrepreneur accepted my proposal and my proposal was implemented in stages. The implementation took two years. To some this may appear a long time. My answer to that is that when problems that have arisen over ten years have been permanently solved in two years, I think the result is at least good, and the entrepreneur thought it was excellent. It is also worth remembering that this solution will enable the company to continue to develop and grow in line with its objectives without fear of further financial problems, provided, of course, that the company adheres to the culture we have developed and implemented together involving the financial management of the company with the help of change drivers.

When I look at the root causes of the financial problems of the company I described above, my general experience is as follows. The company was not managed according to financial objectives, but was driven by customer reactions to its offerings and customer feedback on its performance, rather than by a strategy for the company's performance, which was not, of course, set out by the board of directors. In the absence of a method of financial management of the firm using change drivers, the growth of the firm, the use of resources and the use of the firm's capacity were not managed according to the principles of change drivers for financial management of the firm. As a result of all this, the increase in the total indirect costs of the company in relation to the increase in the total direct costs had become far too high. When the increase in sales and the increase in sales prices could not compensate for the excessive increase in indirect costs, the company was in financial difficulties. Looking at the company's financial difficulties from a different angle, it can also be put like this. The company's management lacked a systematic focus on objectives, and decisions were taken on the basis of subjective feelings and speculation, without any concrete knowledge of the impact of the decisions taken on the company's finances.

PROFITABILITY MONITORING

In order for a company to implement financial management with change drivers to achieve its objectives, it must have accurate and adequate performance monitoring in place as part of its operational management. In particular, this is about monitoring the company's profitability so that it shows how well the company has been able to achieve its profitability objectives. It is not sufficient for operational management to have profitability monitoring in place for the whole company, it must be put in place by the company's operational management on an item-by-item basis. This requires the operational management of the company to define the necessary accounting objects of the company for which the operational management of the enterprise needs to have information about the profitability and the development of the company, in order to enable the operational management of the company to manage the business and its development in an economical way.

Once this has been done, the company will know how its profitability is made up of accounting objects and how changes in the profitability of these accounting objects affect the company's profitability. The objects of calculation for monitoring the profitability of a company must be defined on a company-by- company basis and on the basis of their situation and needs. The following is a list of typical profitability monitoring activities from which the operational management of a company can select those necessary for the business of the company they manage:

1. Actual profitability figures by company
   The actual profitability figures by company show how profitable the companies' businesses are individually and

collectively. This is particularly important for companies with the same owner(s), when the companies are not part of the same group and when the businesses are similar.

2. Actual profitability figures by customer
   The actual profitability figures by customer provide an indication of the profitability of the company's business by customer. This is particularly important for companies that deliver projects for their clients, such as subcontractors to construction companies.

3. Actual profitability figures by order
   The actual profitability figures show how the company's business is performing on a project-by-project basis. This is particularly important for companies that deliver projects for their customers, such as construction companies.

4. Realised profitability figures by tender
   The actual profitability figures by tender show how much of the tender price has been discounted during the bidding phase and how much this has affected the actual profitability of the contract awarded on the basis of the tender. In addition, this analysis can be done by vendor. This analysis is particularly important for companies that deliver projects to their customers, for example, companies that deliver installation projects.

5. Realised profitability figures by region
   The actual profitability figures provide an indication of the profitability of the company's business by region. This is particularly important for companies that provide cleaning services to their customers, for example.

6. Actual profitability figures by product
   The actual profitability figures show how profitable the company's business is by product. This is particularly important both for companies that buy products and resell

them, and for companies that either manufacture products of their own design or manufacture products under licence.

7. Actual profitability figures by service
   Actual profitability figures provide an indication of the profitability of a company's business by service. This is particularly important for businesses providing services, such as hairdressing salons.

8. Realised profitability figures by person
   The actual profitability figures show the profitability of the company's business per person. This is particularly important for businesses where individuals alone provide services to their customers, such as businesses providing maintenance services.

9. Actual profitability figures by machine/vehicle
   The actual profitability figures show the profitability of a company's business by machine/vehicle. This is particularly important, for example, for companies providing excavator services or transport services.

10. Actual profitability figures by subcontractor
    This is particularly important where the company uses subcontractors in its business who provide the same services as the company itself. This is often the case in situations where the firm's own capacity is stretched during peak demand periods and the firm needs the services of subcontractors to supply its customers with the services they have ordered. This is particularly important for transport companies and other service providers.

11. Actual profitability figures by activity
    The company's activities in this context are marketing, sales, production, finance and management. It is generally not appropriate to allocate the income of the company to the functions of the company. In the case of sales, revenues are often allocated by salesperson in order to determine

how much each salesperson has generated in sales. For this reason, the actual profitability figures by function are not about the profitability of the firm by function, but are about cost monitoring, i.e. how well the actual costs of each function compare with the target costs. These figures are the basis for the efficiency analysis of the activities by function.

ACCOUNTING OBJECTS AND COST CENTRES

What are the accounting objects and cost centres?

Accounting objects, or cost centres, are monitoring objects that allow the financial monitoring of a company to be broken down into smaller units. Accounting objects are used to track the related revenues and costs. For example, the profitability of the products and services produced by a company can be monitored by accounting object.

What is the purpose of the accounting objects?

Companies keep statutory accounts and prepare statutory financial statements for the company as a whole, but there is a need for disaggregated profit and loss figures to support operational management of the company. Company accounting is carried out by accounting for all accounting transactions, i.e. revenues and expenses, in accordance with the company-wide chart of accounts, so that they are allocated as desired in the company's accounts and financial statements. The accounting transactions thus accounted for do not yet allow the monitoring and reporting necessary for the management of the company by its operational management. For this reason, accounting objects must be defined for the company, assigned identifiers and allocated to the company's revenues and costs at the same time as the accounting entries are made. On the basis of the information on the accounting objects, the company's electronic financial management information system carries out a target calculation, the results of which are used to generate the operational monitoring reports that the company wants and defines.

What are the benefits of using accounting objects?

It makes it easier to monitor, analyse and compare the revenues and costs of different parts of the business. As with a company's revenues and costs, it is useful to look at profitability from several angles. This requires that the profitability of the company can be viewed in terms of the components whose profitability is being monitored. Once this is done, the company no longer has to guess which parts of its business are the most profitable and which are the least profitable. In order to support the operational management of the enterprise, the financial statements will help the management to identify which parts of the company's business have achieved their defined objectives and which have not, and the extent of the deviations. In addition, the analysis of the financial statements provides a rough indication of the causes of the company's deviations from its targets. When a company uses change drivers in addition to accounting objects, it will know in detail the root causes of its deviations and will be able to draw up more precise and concrete action plans to correct the deviations than would be possible without the use of change drivers.

How to define the accounting objects for a company?

You should define a sufficient number of accounting objects for your company. The company should only define accounting objects according to what the operational management of the company needs to monitor in order to manage the company. In particular, it is important to define a sufficient number of accounting objects whose profitability and development in relation to the objectives the company's management wants to monitor.

How do I define identifiers for the calculation objects?

In order to be able to track the results of the accounting objects that a company wants to track separately, for example by product, by service and by customer, it must be possible to allocate the company's revenues and costs to these accounting objects. Once this is done, the company will be able to monitor profitability and its development, for example by product. However, to achieve this, it must be possible to allocate the company's revenues and costs in parallel to the different objects of calculation. How this can be done in practice depends on the electronic information systems used by the company. It should be borne in mind that this is not possible with all the electronic information systems on the market.

One possible way of separating the company's revenues and costs by accounting objects, for example by product, service and customer, is to define an accounting object allocator. It defines identifiers by product, by service and by customer. A sufficient number of characters are defined for each accounting object ID to allow the allocation of revenues and costs to the correct products. The company must use an invoice item allocator consisting of the identifiers of all the desired invoice items in sequence. For example, a company's accounting object allocator could be in the form: two characters for products, two characters for services and three characters for customers, i.e. in this case the company's accounting object allocator is seven characters long.

What are the constraints on the use of accounting objects?

It is important to note that the use of a company's electronic information systems is limited by the number of accounting objects the company wishes to use, i.e. the number of accounting objects the company's accounting object allocator can contain. A company should use an electronic financial management system and other necessary electronic information systems that can handle the number of accounting objects in the accounting object allocator that the company requires. Some electronic financial management systems on the market allow only numbers to be used in the accounting object allocator, i.e. the accounting object identifiers it contains, and other electronic financial management systems allow letters and combinations of letters to be used in addition to numbers. Another important aspect of a company's electronic financial management system is the automation built into it to facilitate the use of the accounting cursor. In practice, this means that it is not necessary to define in the accounting object cursor all the cursor characters for each revenue (income) and each cost (expenditure), but it is sufficient to define the characters for one accounting object identifier, and the electronic information system automation will define the rest of the accounting object cursor characters. In addition, electronic information systems nowadays use artificial intelligence and robotics, for example, which learn routine human tasks so that they can be transferred to a robot – account entries, for instance. An example is a company that produces projects using machines, and wants to track, on a machine-by-machine basis, the profitability of the machines used to produce the projects. Once it is defined in the electronic information system which machine is used for each project, it is sufficient to define a project ID in the company's accounting object allocator, so that the income or cost of the project is allocated to both the project and the machine used in the project.

What should be taken into account when defining the calculation targets?

It is very important that each company has access to the accounting objects that the company really needs. When designing and defining the calculation objects, it is important to be sensible so as not to choose unnecessary calculation objects and to avoid making their use too cumbersome and burdensome. Unnecessary calculation objects increase the amount of work required to use them and cause unnecessary costs for the company.

The use of calculation objects should only provide the company with information that is useful for the operational management of the company. In general, it is worthwhile to introduce monitoring items that can really be influenced by the company.

The definition of targets is always company-specific.

PRICING

The price of products and services on the market is determined by what customers are willing to pay for them. This results in market prices for products and services. A company's business must be able to make the necessary changes on an ongoing basis so that it can continually achieve its objectives as the market prices of its products and services change, and as the characteristics of the products and services and the volume of demand change.

When a firm manufactures or buys products for sale or produces services (including projects) for sale, before determining their selling prices the firm must know the direct costs incurred by the firm, by product, for their manufacture, the costs of purchasing and buying the products purchased and, by service, the costs of producing them. In addition to these costs, the selling prices per product and per service must include the related indirect costs:

From production

From marketing

From sales

From management

From financial management

From the company, fixed costs, depreciation and financial charges and target coverage based on the company's budget objectives

The result of these measures is the definition of the target sales prices for each product and service. For start-ups, these figures are either based on experience or other estimates. For existing businesses, these figures are derived from past performance, provided that they are collected in the right way and are sufficiently accurate. Before setting sales prices, these costs must take account of the need for changes to achieve the company's budget, since sales prices cannot be determined solely on the basis of the previous year's figures.

When a product or service is sold only once, the company must be able to price its direct and indirect costs accurately enough on the basis of experience, and by no means on a purely guesswork basis, so that once the orders have been received, their realisation is not left to chance, with the risk of getting into financial difficulties as a result of pricing errors.

The collection of information on the realisation of direct and, in particular, indirect costs by business activity, either by product or by service in existing companies, must be planned and implemented on a case-by-case basis with sufficient precision and in an economically sound manner.

In addition to the above, when pricing your products and services, it is worth remembering that ultimately it is the customers who decide on the prices of your products and services in the context of their purchasing behaviour. In the light of what we have said above about cost-oriented pricing, a firm has the option of pricing its products and services either on the basis of the benefits to the customer or on the basis of the firm's spare capacity.

Once the seller has identified the economic benefits that the buyer will receive when buying the company's product or service, the seller can price the product or service so that when the customer buys the product or service, the customer will receive the economic benefits that the customer seeks and the selling company will receive an exceptionally high margin on the transaction, i.e. both parties win. In my experience, when the seller knows what the customer will get when buying the product or service sold by the seller, it is very easy for the seller to close the deal when he can tell the buyer the specific criteria and reasons for buying the product or service that is being sold.

The practice of pricing a company's products and services on the basis of spare capacity has increased markedly in recent years. In particular, there has been an increase in the pricing of air travel, bus travel and transport services. In the case of air fares and bus fares, the price of a trip peaks immediately after the trip is announced and then falls until the time of departure, depending on how close the time of purchase is to the time of departure, and also on the number of seats available on the aircraft or bus at the time of purchase. In transport pricing, capacity pricing is typically based either on available pallet metres or on available pallet cubes. When a seller sells a transport service from A to B to a customer, there is spare capacity left on the transport vehicle both on the outward journey and especially on the return journey. In such cases, the seller sets the price for the first customer in each case so that the selling price covers all the costs of the transport. When the seller then sells the spare capacity for this transport service, he reduces the selling price of the spare capacity as the additional load is taken on board. In all three of these free capacity pricing systems, unit prices are variable rather than fixed. The objective is to maximise the total amount of euros that the seller receives for the goods and services sold, i.e. the maximum total margin in relation to the total price.

OPERATIONAL PROFIT AND LOSS ACCOUNT

Purpose of the operating profit and loss account

The external accounting includes income statement and balance sheet reporting to the company's external stakeholders. External stakeholders include tax authorities, other public authorities and investors. Financial statements and tax-related reports are the main outputs of external accounting. The income statement and balance sheet are mainly for the tax authorities. The external accounting of the company does not adequately serve the operational management of the company. That is why, for the financial management of the company, I have developed principles for the preparation of the company's operational profit and loss accounts.

Principle of the operating profit and loss account

In the CHANGE DRIVER method of change management, the operational profit and loss account includes at a rough level: revenues, direct costs, indirect costs and profit and loss figures. These need to be defined in more detail on a company-by-company basis, taking into account the situation of the company and its needs.

At a general level, a company's operating profit and loss account should include the following accounts of the operating profit and loss account:

1. Revenue from sales

2. Direct costs of production

3. Indirect costs of production

4. **Margin on sales from production**

5. Marketing costs

6. Cost of sales

7. Financial management costs

8. Management costs

9. Other common costs

10. Fixed costs

11. **Operating margin**

12. Depreciation

13. Operating result

14. Financial income and expenses

15. Profit before accounting transfers and taxes

16. Accounting transfers

17. Taxes

18. Profit for the financial year

Sales revenue refers to the revenue from the sale of the company's core business. Sales revenue does not include the presence of a gaming machine in the entrance hall of a manufacturing company from which the enterprise derives revenue.

The activities of the company are marketing, sales, production, finance and management. The costs in the operating profit and loss account include all the costs of each activity, e.g. wage costs and other activity costs.

In the CHANGE DRIVER method of change management, the income and expenses of a company's operational profit and loss account are divided into direct and indirect as follows:

1. All sales revenues related to the core operational business of the company are direct revenues.

2. Direct costs associated with the operational business of the company are the direct costs of production.

3. The indirect costs of the company are treated separately in two categories, namely:

    3.1 Indirect costs linked to the operational business of the company, which are:

3.1.1 Indirect costs of production

3.1.2 Marketing costs

3.1.3 Cost of sales

3.1.4 Financial management costs

3.1.5 Management costs

3.2 Indirect costs related to the non-operational business of the company, which are:

3.2.1 Other common costs

3.2.2 Fixed costs

3.2.3 Depreciation (imputed costs)

3.2.4 Financial income and expenses

3.2.5 Transfers for accounting purposes

The above division between direct and indirect income and expenditure of the company is of particular relevance when determining the change drivers for the company.

Subcontracting

There are two types of subcontracting that a company can have in its business:

1. Subcontracting related to the company's own production

2. Subcontracting that complements the company's own production

The company's own production is typically either the manufacture of products in production, or the production of solutions in projects on the customer's premises. In this case, the manufacture of products and the production of solutions for projects are assembly operations. In assembly, the company needs parts that the company has decided, for one reason or another, to buy from a subcontractor and not to produce them itself. The most common reason for this decision is that the subcontractor is able to produce the parts more cheaply than the company can produce them in-house. In these cases, the subcontracting is related to the company's own production.

Subcontracting, which complements a firm's own production, means that the firm has its own production either for the manufacture of the firm's products or for the services provided by the firm. The services may also be projects. Typically, the more the demand for the products manufactured by the firm and the services provided by the firm varies, the more firms will want to subcontract to suppliers to supplement their own production. This requires that the subcontractor is able to produce the same products and/or services as the firm. In doing so, the firm aims to produce the basic demand, i.e. the smallest possible share of demand, in its own production, thereby bringing its own production capacity to the smallest possible load and at the same time to the highest possible level of utilisation, thus making the best use of the firm's production capacity. In these situations, the firm buys in products and services from a subcontractor to meet the firm's peak demand for its products and services. At the same time, it is worth noting that subcontracting that complements the firm's own production is at the same time subcontracting that competes with the firm's own production. In these cases, the subcontracting is complementary to the firm's own production.

In the case of subcontracting related to a company's own production, the costs of subcontracting are direct costs of production in the operating profit and loss account. These subcontracting costs should be recorded under a separate account number in order to reflect these costs in the operational profit and loss account.

In the case of subcontracting that complements the company's own production, the figures relating to the company's own production and the figures relating to subcontracting that complements the company's own production should be shown separately in the profit and loss account up to the level of the profit margin. In addition, the profit and loss account must include the total production sales margin, which includes both the sales margin from the company's own production and the sales margin from subcontracting activities complementing the company's own production.

Internal services

Internal services are those internal services that are necessary to enable the company's production to function as intended. It must be possible to allocate the costs of internal services sufficiently directly to the products and services produced by the company. A typical internal service provided by companies is maintenance services. The costs of maintenance services are either direct costs or indirect costs. One of the key objectives is to be able to provide internal services efficiently and effectively at the lowest possible indirect cost, as defined by the company's internal customer, i.e. production. Internal services may have been developed by the company on the basis of its own needs or internalised by the company's purchasing them from a service provider. If the internal services are not provided cost-effectively enough by the company in the manner specified by production, then the internal services are typically outsourced from the company.

The costs of internal services must be shown separately in the company's operating profit and loss account under indirect costs of production. The number of accounts for internal services should be defined on the basis of the needs of the company and should be sufficient to provide sufficient detail of the costs. In the operating profit and loss account, the costs of the internal services of the company should be shown broken down into direct costs and indirect costs.

Processes

In my third book, "RESURSSIEN TULOKSILLA YRITYKSEN TAVOITE-TULOKSEEN", I have described the business processes and explained how to describe them, so I will not go into them again here. Here I will describe the company's processes from the perspective of how they relate to the financial management of the company through change drivers. Processes consist of a chain of interrelated steps. Each stage of a process contains a set of tasks that must be performed in each stage of the process in accordance with the objectives, so that the process can produce outputs in accordance with the objectives from the inputs made. In this context, a company's activities always consist of two types of processes, which are:

1. Processes that are formed by the interrelationship of the activities of the company.

2. The processes within the company's activities.

Whatever the business of the company, the business functions of the company are: production, marketing, sales, finance and management. The production functions are divided into two activities, direct production and indirect production. It is necessary to define all the processes of the company, but for the financial management of the company with change drivers, only the core processes of the function need to be defined. As a general rule, each activity of a company has one core process, but there may be more than one. Before defining the core processes of a company function, it is necessary to identify who the customer or customers of each function are. Although in all companies the customer base of the functions is the same, irrespective of the company's business, this issue should be discussed on a company-by-company basis, as in each company at least the external customers of the company are different. The customers of a company's activities are:

1. The customers of a firm's direct production are the final customers of the products and services produced by the firm.

2. The customers of the indirect production of the company are the direct production of the enterprise.

3. The customers of the firm's sales are the indirect production.

4. The customer of the firm's marketing is sales.

5. The customer of the financial management of the company is the management.

6. The management of the enterprise is the customer of all the above-mentioned activities of the company.

It is very important to be aware that the customers of the company's activities define the requirements, criteria and needs for change for the services provided by the activities and their development. All too often companies have forgotten this principle, in a way, by remaining at the level of opinion: "Customers come and go. These are the customers we have at the moment".

When it comes to defining the internal processes of a company, it is best to focus on the essentials, i.e. defining the core process of each function in the company. Over the years, I have seen a large number of pictures and definitions of company processes in my client companies. The pictures made in companies are too detailed and complex because they are usually made for the company's quality system. As such, they are not suitable as a basis for the financial management of a company with change drivers. At activity level, there are often only four steps in the core processes of individual activities. The following are examples.

An example of a core marketing process:

Step 1:   Defining and identifying key customers (suspects)

Step 2:   Awareness raising (company and its products and services)

Step 3:   Finding potential customers (prospecting, prospecting, prospecting) or prospects

Step 4:   Warming up prospects for sales

An example of a core sales process:

    Step 1:   Meeting prospects

    Step 2:   Making proposals to prospects

    Step 3:   Negotiating with prospects

    Step 4:   Closing deals

An example of a direct core production process:

    Step 1:   Material transfers

    Step 2:   Component assembly

    Step 3:   Assembly and finishing

    Step 4:   Delivery

An example of an indirect core production process:

    Step 1:   Splitting production orders into material procurement and resource utilisation

    Step 2:   Ensuring material availability on an order-by-order basis to fulfil the orders

    Step 3:   Ensuring, on an order-by-order basis, the use of resources to fulfil the orders

    Step 4:   Planning and communicating the production programme for orders

An example of a core management process:

Step 1:   Defining and committing to objectives.

Step 2:   Action planning and budgeting

Step 3:   Operational management

Step 4:   Service management

For a company, the core processes of financial management are:

> Invoicing

> Payment

> Payroll

> Reporting

Once the company's processes have been defined by function, and the results of the monitoring of the analysis of the company's activities at the level of the functions are known, the company has been able to introduce financial management at the level of the company's functions with change drivers. In practice, this means that the results produced by the company's activities are monitored (by monitoring the output of the company's activities). Based on the needs of the company, the use of change drivers in procurement for the financial management of the company can be extended to the level of the stages of the operational processes of the company's activities. In practice, this can be done in the following way.

Based on the above, the core processes of the company's functions and the change drivers in use at the level of those functions, by function, are known. As a result of the analysis of the company's activities, the company has previously had access to a list of work to be done in each of these activities. This list can now be used by the company to analyse the need for the work, the methods used to carry it out and the results of the work at each stage of its core processes by function. The performance of each stage of the core processes of the company's activities can also be monitored and analysed by means of output monitoring.

Outsourcing and internalisation

In this context, outsourcing means selling a company's business or part of its business to a supplier outside the company. By outsourcing, I mean buying the business or part of the business of an external service provider as part of the company's business. In this context, I refer to outsourcing and internalisation of business activities of companies collectively as business transfers. In what follows, profitable business is defined as a business in which the firm's profitability objectives are met. On the other hand, by unprofitable business I mean a business in which the profitability targets set for the firm are not met.

Why do companies outsource and insource their business activities?

The general rationale for business transfers is that unprofitable businesses are outsourced and profitable businesses are internalised. When a company outsources an unprofitable business, the buyer believes that it can turn it into a profitable business or that the buyer will obtain synergies from the purchase that will make the acquired business profitable. The internalisation of a business, on the other hand, typically involves the company believing that the service it buys from an external supplier is expensive, that by buying that service the business buyer believes that it will gain an economic benefit from the transaction.

I think that business transfers represent one way and one opportunity for companies to develop their business. In this context, I would like to warn against using business transfers to achieve uncontrolled growth of companies. Uncontrolled growth is when an unprofitable company buys a business and is unable to use it to improve its profitability; in the worst cases, the profitability of the buying company's business may deteriorate. A company consisting of unprofitable businesses is not profitable. If one business of a firm is unprofitable, then it is always the unprofitable business that erodes the profitability of the firm's other businesses. In my experience, when all of a firm's businesses are profitable, the growth potential for improving the firm's profitability is greater than the sum of the profitability of the firm's businesses. In other words, when the profitable businesses of a company work together, the company's business will benefit from synergies to achieve profitability growth. Conversely, when unprofitable businesses operate together, synergy disadvantages arise for the firm to increase the unprofitable ones.

It is very important to keep the following principle in mind. When a principal financially manages the business for which he is responsible in accordance with the lessons of this book, and when a subordinate acts in accordance with the lessons and opportunities of this book, the result is a business that always achieves its financial objectives. Who owns the business at any given time is not the core issue for either the principal or the subordinate. For them, the core issue is that there will always be buyers for a business that will always achieve its financial goals, and there will always be demand in the market for the people who can make it happen. For their own careers, they should gather concrete evidence of what they have done, how they have done it and what results they have been able to achieve. Fears and threats disappear and turn into opportunities when you do the right thing!

BUDGETING

The target structure of the company's operating income and expenditure is defined at the budgeting stage by defining the structure of the company's operational profit and loss account. The accounts in the operating profit and loss account are intended to remain the same from one year to the next in order to achieve continuity. It is essential in the operating profit and loss account that no attempt is made to allocate indirect costs of production, marketing, sales, financial administration and management costs or other common costs, fixed costs, financial income and financial charges to the products and services produced by the company. When targets for these costs are defined in the target operating statement, it is also known how each target figure differs from the actual figure in the previous year's operating statement. This variance represents the need to amend this chapter in order to meet the company's budget in this respect. The company's activities are marketing, sales, production, finance and management. The costs of the activities include all the costs of each activity, e.g. wages and salaries and other expenses of the activity. When the figures of the actual operating profit and loss account of the previous year are known, e.g. direct and indirect costs in production, marketing costs, sales costs, financial administration costs and management costs, then the actual costs of each of the company's activities are known, i.e. how much the services provided by each of these activities cost in total, i.e. the total actual cost of the services provided by the operational process of each of these activities (output costs).

In order to be able to use change drivers for the financial management of a company, an operational profit and loss account for the previous financial year must be available. Budgeting for the following year should be done in the form of an operational profit and loss account, which should be prepared in a way that meets the performance targets set by the owner of the company. In this case, the basis for the company's budgeting for the following financial year is the operational profit and loss account, which contains rough figures for the company's change requirements. For the previous financial year, the profitability figures for the previous financial year, taking into account the business activities of the company, are still required, for example, by product, service, project, resource (people and machines) and customer. Once the target figures for the changes needed to achieve the company's budget are known, the next step is to analyse the possibilities for change within the company to achieve the target figures, i.e. what the possible means are and what their impact on the company's results will be. In practice, this means considering the answers to the following questions:

1. To what extent can the prices of a company's products and services be changed and what is their impact on the company's performance?

2. To what extent can the sales volumes of the firm's products and services be changed without investment and what is their potential impact on the firm's performance?

3. To what extent can the direct costs and direct operations of the firm's products and services be made more efficient and productive without investment, and what is their potential impact on the firm's performance?

4. To what extent is it possible to bring about changes in the indirect costs of the firm, i.e. how can the efficiency and productivity of the firm's indirect activities be increased and what is their potential impact on the firm's performance?

5. To what extent can the free capacity of the company's resources (people and machines) be used in the company and what is their impact on the company's performance?

6. To what extent can the firm produce and sell new products and services and what is their impact on the firm's performance?

7. To what extent does the firm need to make new investments and what is their impact on the firm's performance?

8. To what extent can the firm change the structure of its business, for example through outsourcing and mergers and acquisitions, and what is the potential impact of a change in the structure of the firm's business on its performance?

9. When seeking answers to the above questions, it is useful to use the above profitability figures for the previous financial year.

Once the company has the answers to these questions, the next step is to choose and decide which of the possible change agents identified in the answers to these questions will be implemented during the budget period, and how much each change agent is intended to improve the company's performance as part of the changes required to achieve the company's budget.

Once the company has selected the means of change and decided on their impact, the next step is to implement them and to identify the people responsible for them, who will have to draw up concrete, measurable and easy-to-follow action plans for implementing the changes.

CHANGE DRIVERS

What are change drivers?

In my second book, "RESURSSIEN TULOKSILLA YRITYKSEN TAVOITETULOKSEEN", I have answered this question by saying "What is the purpose of change drivers?" and "What does it take for a company to implement change drivers?"

Change drivers are performance measures used in a company to measure the impact of operational changes on the company's performance.

Another definition of change drivers is as follows:

The use of change drivers makes the objectives of a company's performance changes and the planning and monitoring of the implementation of the measures required to achieve them more concrete.

Change drivers directly related to the operational profit and loss account of the company are:

1. Change drivers related to the incomes and direct costs of the company:

    1.1 Drivers of change in selling prices

    1.2 Drivers of change in sales volume

    1.3 Drivers of change in direct costs of production

    1.4 Drivers of change in the direct efficiency of production drivers

    1.5 Drivers of change in capacity utilisation of direct production resources (machinery and persons)

2. Indirect drivers of change related to the non-operational business of the company:

    2.1 Drivers of change in other common costs

    2.2 Variation drivers for fixed costs

    2.3 Variation drivers for depreciation and amortisation

    2.4 Drivers of change in financial income and charges

    2.5 Deductions for changes in financial transactions

The company's functions are production, marketing, sales, finance and management. Marketing, sales, finance and management are the internal service providers for the production of the company, enabling the company's production to operate in accordance with its objectives. In the same way, indirect production activities, such as production planning and work management, are providers of internal services to the direct production of the company. For this reason, in a company's operating profit and loss account, the costs of production are divided into direct and indirect costs in the profit and loss account. In order to examine separately the costs of internal services and their evolution, they are presented separately in the company's operating profit and loss account as follows:

1. Indirect production costs

2. Total marketing costs

3. Total cost of sales

4. Total financial management costs

5. Total cost of management

These costs represent the total cost of the operational process of each internal service-providing activity within the company. The following change drivers are associated with the provision of internal services:

1. Change drivers for indirect production costs

2. Change drivers for total marketing costs

3. Change drivers for the total cost of sales

4. Change drivers for the total cost of financial management

5. Change drivers for total management costs

For each activity, target values are defined for the cost change drivers, either at the activity level or, where appropriate, at the activity's operational process stage level, during budgeting, based on either the need for a change in capacity utilisation or the need for a change in cost-effectiveness or both.

In order to achieve the targeted performance impacts of changes in the business structure of the company, such as business outsourcing or mergers, it is also possible and appropriate to define change drivers, but these will not be discussed here due to their specific case-by-case nature.

Change drivers in budgeting

It is very important that only essential change drivers are used from one financial year to the next and that, as a rule, change drivers are only changed when a company needs to make a substantial strategic change in business direction. Before target figures can be set for change drivers in the budgeting process, these change drivers must have actual figures for the previous financial year.

Before defining targets for the change drivers of the company's activities in budgeting, the following points should be noted:

1. Cost changes resulting from changes in the direct production of the company have a direct impact on the operational profit and loss account of the company and its result.

2. The changes in costs resulting from changes in internal services, i.e. indirect production, marketing, sales, financial management and management, have a direct impact on the operating profit and loss account of the company and its result. It should be borne in mind that, for all internal service activities, the service content requirements, service criteria and related change needs for budgeting purposes are defined by the internal service customers.

When setting target figures for the budgeting of internal service activities, it is possible to do so on the basis of either economic benefits or cost-effectiveness in the following alternative ways:

1. Change drivers that have a direct impact on the company's performance. The change drivers that have a direct impact on the firm's profit at the level of the sales margin are:

    - Sales price change drivers, e.g. the direct impact on the firm's performance of a 1% change in sales price.

    - A change in sales volume, e.g. the direct effect on the firm's performance of one product sold.

    - Drivers of change in direct costs of production, e.g. the direct effect on the company's profit of a 1% increase in fuel costs or a 1% decrease in purchase prices for production.

    - Drivers of change in the direct efficiency of production, e.g. the direct effect on the firm's performance of a 1% saving in working time.

    - Drivers of change in the utilisation rate of direct production resources (machinery and persons), e.g. the direct effect of a 1% utilisation rate on the profit of the company.

Once the immediate need for a change in the company's sales margin is known, the next step is to select the most appropriate change drivers for the company's situation from those described above and use them to determine which changes in the change drivers will be used to achieve the targeted change in the budget's sales margin.

The following is an example of defining a change driver for the capacity utilisation rate of a firm's direct production resources (machines and persons): KKMD = 100 x VKM / KOK

KKMD = Capacity utilisation rate of direct resources (machinery and persons) of the production of the company [%] is the percentage change in capacity utilisation rate.

VKM = Free capacity change [h].

KOK = Available capacity [h].

The effect on the firm's performance of a change in the capacity utilisation rate of the firm's direct production resources (machinery and persons) can then be calculated as follows:

KKMSOVYT = KKMD x KH

KKMSOVYT = The effect on the firm's profit of a change in the capacity utilisation rate of the firm's direct production resources (machinery and persons) [€].

KKMD = Change in the capacity utilisation rate of the direct production resources of the company (machinery and persons) [%] is the percentage change in the capacity utilisation rate.

KH = Capacity cost of the company in euros per percentage of capacity utilisation [€/%].

2. Drivers of change in intra-company services and their impact on company performance

When defining the activities that generate intra-corporate services, i.e. for:

1. Indirect production

2. Marketing

3. Sales

4. Financial management

5. Management

Change drivers can either be change drivers that directly affect the company's performance, e.g. change drivers of sales prices negotiated by sales, change drivers of sales volume of goods and services produced by the company sold by sales, change drivers of production purchases made by indirect production, change drivers of total costs of operations, or change drivers that indirectly affect the company's performance. The change drivers indirectly affecting the performance of the enterprise are the change drivers whose changes affect the output of each service within the company. Changes in internal services also have a direct impact on the performance of the company.

When defining the drivers of change for the internal service activities of a company, it is a question of the efficiency and cost-effectiveness of each internal service activity. Internal services produce the following outputs:

1. Marketing generates the number of prospects.

2. Sales produce the number of transactions, the number of transactions in units and in euros.

3. Indirect production produces the number of production orders received and the change in production purchase prices.

4. Management produces servant management (for more information on servant management, see my third book: "RESURSSIEN TULOKSILLA YRITYKSEN TAVOITETULOKSEEN"), i.e. based on the needs of the function, for example:

    a. The number of prospectuses.

    b. Number of shops and euros.

c. Reduce the total cost of operations.

d. Reduce the fixed costs of the business.

e. Affects the firm's depreciation costs.

f. Affects the financial income and costs of the company.

g. Helps the firm's activities to improve their operating efficiency, for example, to increase the quantity of outputs produced by the activities in a time unit [units/hour].

h. Develop new products or services for the company. The value in euros of new products in improving the company's performance is determined on a case-by-case basis.

i. Provide training for change, the value in euros of which in terms of improving the performance of the company is determined on a case-by-case basis.

j. Outsource or internalise (= sell or buy) businesses into the company. The euro value of these effects in terms of improving the performance of the company is determined on a case-by-case basis.

k. To enter into business combinations. The euro value of these effects on the improvement of the performance of the company is determined on a case-by-case basis.

Above, we have considered the definition of change drivers for internal services at the level of the services provided by the core processes of internal services. If necessary, companies can define the change drivers for internal services at the level of each stage of the core internal service processes of the company similarly to the above. This is particularly necessary when there is a need to "turn over a new leaf", i.e. dig out all the potential for improving the performance of the company.

When you want to include in the direct costs of production the total costs of employees' cost hours that are not allocated to products or services provided to customers, one effective way to do this is to add these costs separately to the indirect costs of production. In this way, these costs can be used as an additional driver of cost-effectiveness change in the firm's production. In budgeting, when target figures are defined for change drivers related to the costs of internal service-producing activities on the basis of the need to change the cost-effectiveness of the activity phase, it is a question of changing the number of working hours used by the company's resources (people and machines) in relation to the number of outputs produced by the activity. An example of improving cost-effectiveness is when the same number of outputs can be produced in a work phase by using fewer working hours to perform them.

The following is an example of the definition of a change driver for the reduction of the number of hours worked in one phase of an intra-corporate service activity:

$$TVKK = TKK \times TVKT / TKKTMY$$

TVKK = Total cost of a phase of an activity [€]

TKK = Total cost of the operation [€].

TVKT = Hours spent on the activity phase [h], i.e. the number before the change

TKKTY = Total hours spent on the activity [h], i.e. the number before the change

The impact on the firm's performance of a change in the number of hours worked in one phase of the intra-corporate services activity can then be calculated as follows:

$$TVKMSOYT = TVKK \times TVKTMD / TVKT$$

TVKMSOVYT = The impact on the company's result of a change in the number of hours spent on a phase of the activity [€].

TVKK = Total cost of the operation phase [€]

TVKTMD = The change in the number of hours spent on a phase [h].

TVKT = Hours worked [h], i.e. the number before the change

3. Business change taxes by accounting object

In the context of corporate budgeting, it is also useful to look at the profitability of the company's chosen accounting objects for the previous financial year. It is also worth using change drivers to identify the change needs in the company's accounting objects that are necessary to achieve the objectives of the company's budget. In this context, it is essential to find case-specific answers to the following questions:

3.1 What are the opportunities for change in the actual results of the company's accounting objects in the previous financial year?

3.2 Which of the opportunities for change are selected for inclusion in the budget?

3.3 Which change drivers are chosen from the selected change opportunities to be used? This can be done when detailed actual figures by accounting object are available for the previous financial year. For the selected change options, the objectives, the change drivers needed to achieve the objectives and the measures to be taken to achieve the objectives are defined.

Benefits of the solution

In this book, I have focused in particular on explaining how the change management method of the CHANGE DRIVER should create the conditions for the financial management of a company with change drivers. What follows is a summary of the benefits that can be achieved through this method:

1. The business owners define performance targets for the business for its budgeting, which include at a rough level the financial change needs for the detailed planning of the business budget.

2. The operational budget of the company is presented in the form of an operational profit and loss account, including cost targets by activity.

3. In addition to the company's performance targets, the company's budget planning is based on the results of the previous budget period:

    3.1 Realised operating profit and loss account.

    3.2 Realised profitability figures by accounting object.

    3.3 Realised efficiency figures by activity, by stage of the operational process of the activity and by resource, where appropriate.

    3.4 Realised capacity utilisation rates by resource.

    3.5 Results achieved through the use of change drivers.

4. On the basis of the company's budgeted operational profit and loss account, budget targets are also defined for the accounting objects defined by the company.

5. Based on the objectives of the company's activities,

budgeting can define efficiency objectives for each stage of the operational process of each activity and further for each resource (machine and human). Budgeting also defines objectives for the use of the capacity of the company's resources (machines and people).

6. The actual profit figures for the profitability of the company's business are provided both in the form of an operational profit and loss account and broken down by accounting object, thus identifying, by accounting object, the deviations from the targets, i.e. which accounting objects have not achieved the performance targets set for them. In addition, it is possible to monitor the realisation of the company's capacity utilisation and compare it with the budgeted targets, i.e. to identify, by resource, the deviations in capacity utilisation compared to the budget targets.

7. The actual operational efficiency figures of the company's operational processes, their stages and resources are compared with the targets set for them, except in the company's electronic information systems, because their use would be unnecessarily cumbersome and costly. One good way is to monitor the actual performance of the company's operational processes, steps and resources in Excel, either as output tracking of activities or steps, and to compare the performance against the targets set for budgeting purposes.

8. The budgeting process involves drawing up concrete and detailed action plans for the changes included in the budget, the implementation of which is monitored during the budgeted period. This will allow any negative deviations from the impact of the action plans on the performance figures to be identified at an early stage, so that corrective measures can be planned and implemented without unnecessary delays.

9. The action plans will be drawn up using change drivers, the

use of which will make the results of the measures taken more tangible.

10. The use of change drivers enhances the predictability of the company's performance by having change-driver-specific action plans in place for changes in the performance impact of the change drivers.

11. Management becomes a systematic and concrete activity aimed at achieving objectives, exploiting the potential for efficiency and capacity, and giving all people in the company the opportunity to influence the results through their own actions and to share in the rewards distributed to the company's staff on the basis of the results achieved.

Financial management of the company

Objectives

In this chapter, I will focus on how the financial objectives of a company are implemented throughout the organisation, step by step. I have gone into more detail on the content of these stages in my second book: "RESURSSIEN TULOKSILLA YRITYKSEN TAVOITETULOKSEEN" and in my first book: "KOKO YRITYKSEN KAPASITEETTI TEHOKÄYTTÖÖN". Defining the objectives of a business, including the financial objectives, starts when the business owner sets out a vision for the business. In this context, the definition of the business owner's financial objectives must include, in particular, the definition of the profit objective. This must be the key financial objective of the business, since the business owner has invested his own capital in the business as required and may, if necessary, have provided security for the borrowed capital needed by the business. The entrepreneur must receive a return on the capital invested in his business, so that he retains the financial incentive to continue investing in the business and not to invest this capital in other, more profitable activities. Although a business owner may define non-financial objectives for his business, in this context I would like to emphasise the importance of the financial return of the business in relation to the objectives defined by the business owner.

Once the financial objectives defined by the company owner are known, the next step is to draw up a strategy for the company. The strategy defines the direction of the company's business and the financial milestones to achieve the financial objectives defined by the company owner. Translating a company's strategy into action starts with defining the financial objectives in the strategy. Usually, the strategy of a company is drawn up by the board of directors. For this reason, the board of a company must have a broad knowledge of the markets in which the company operates and a broad and in-depth knowledge of the various aspects of the company's business. The CEO should be involved in the development of the company's strategy, as he or she is responsible for translating the company's financial objectives from the strategy into action. Once the strategy has been drawn up by the board of directors, the board of directors should approve the strategy with the owner of the company, so that the board of directors is also committed to the financial objectives and content of the strategy.

Once a strategy has been defined, the next step is to draw up a business plan for the company. The business plan is the basis for the operational planning of the company's business. The company's business plan is prepared by the company's CEO, who is explicitly responsible for the implementation of the financial and other objectives defined by the company's board of directors in the company's strategy. The business plan should set out the financial objectives for the next three years, based on the company's strategy, and provide a plan for how the company intends to achieve these objectives. Operational financial management of the company must be based on the financial objectives of the company's business plan. Once the business plan has been drawn up, the CEO should present it to the company's board of directors and have it approved by them, so that the CEO can also commit the board of directors to the financial objectives and content of the business plan. However, it should be borne in mind that this procedure does not allow the CEO to reduce, remove or delegate his responsibility for the implementation of the financial objectives set by the board of directors.

Once a business plan has been drawn up for a company, the company's budgeting must be based on it and carried out on a financial year basis. The preparation and implementation of the company's financial objectives and the budgets and action plans to achieve them throughout the company's organisation is the responsibility of the company's CEO, who is responsible for implementing the financial objectives set by the company's board of directors, i.e. the operational management of the company. The following steps should be taken in the budgeting process for the implementation of the company's financial objectives:

1. Financial objectives for the operational profit and loss account of the company.

2. Financial objectives for the company's operations.

3. Financial targets for the operational phases of the company's activities.

4. Economic objectives for the resources of the company.

Just because the CEO is responsible for implementing these financial objectives does not mean that he or she has to do it all alone. In defining these objectives, in defining the change drivers to achieve them and in drawing up action plans to achieve the financial objectives set out in the company's budget, the CEO should draw on the experience and expertise of other managers in the company's organisation. The CEO should therefore delegate the responsibilities and activities related to these activities to other persons in the company at his discretion. How this should be done depends, of course, on the company's situation, the ability of its staff and the need for change within the company's budget.

BUDGETING

The target structure of the company's operating income and expenditure is defined at the budgeting stage by defining the structure of the company's operational profit and loss account. The accounts in the operating profit and loss account are intended to remain the same from one year to the next in order to achieve continuity. It is essential in the operating profit and loss account that no attempt is made to allocate indirect costs of production, marketing, sales, financial administration and management costs, other common costs, fixed costs, financial income and financial charges to the products and services produced by the company. When targets are set for these costs in the target operating profit and loss account, it is also known how each target figure differs from the actual figure in the previous year's operating profit and loss account. This variance represents the need for a change in that figure in order for the company's budget to be achieved in this respect. The company's functions are marketing, sales, production, finance and management. The costs of the activities include all the costs of each activity, e.g. wages and salaries and other costs of the activity. When the figures of the previous year's actual operating profit and loss account are known, e.g. direct and indirect costs in production, marketing costs, sales costs, financial administration costs and management costs, then the actual costs of each of the company's activities are known, i.e. how much the services provided by each of these activities cost in total, i.e. the total actual cost of the services provided by the operational process of each of these activities (output costs).

In order to be able to use change drivers for the financial management of a company, an operational profit and loss account for the previous financial year must be available. Budgeting for the following year should be done in the form of an operational profit and loss account, which should be prepared in a way that meets the performance targets set by the owner of the company. In this case, the basis for the company's budgeting for the following financial year is the operational profit and loss account, which contains rough figures for the change requirements of the company.

For the previous financial year, depending on the company's business, the profitability figures for the previous financial year are also required – for example, by product, service, project, resource (people and machines) and customer. Once the target figures for the changes required to achieve the company's budget are known, the next step is to analyse the possibilities for change within the company to achieve the target figures, i.e. what the possible means are and what their impact on the company's results will be. In practice, this means considering the answers to the following questions:

1. To what extent can the prices of a company's products and services be changed and what is their impact on the company's performance?

2. To what extent can the sales volumes of the firm's products and services be changed without investment and what is their potential impact on the firm's performance?

3. To what extent can the direct costs and direct operations of the firm's products and services be made more efficient and productive without investment, and what is their potential impact on the firm's performance?

4. To what extent can changes be made in the indirect costs of the firm, i.e. how can the efficiency and productivity of the firm's indirect activities be increased, and what is their potential impact on the firm's performance?

5. To what extent can the spare capacity of the firm's resources (people and machines) be used within the firm and what is their potential impact on the firm's performance?

6. To what extent can the firm produce and sell new products

and services and what is their potential impact on the firm's performance?

7. To what extent does the company need to make new investments, and what is their impact on the company's performance?

8. To what extent can a firm change the structure of its business, for example through outsourcing and mergers and acquisitions, and what is the potential impact of a change in the firm's business structure on its performance?

9. When seeking answers to the above questions, it is useful to use the profitability figures for the previous financial year.

Once the company has the answers to these questions, the next step is to choose and decide which of the possible change agents identified in the answers to these questions will be implemented during the budget period and how much each change agent is intended to improve the company's performance as part of the changes required to achieve the company's budget.

Once the company has selected the means of change and decided on their impact, the next step is to implement them and to identify the people responsible for them, who will have to draw up concrete, measurable and easy-to-follow action plans for implementing the changes.

CHANGE MEASURES TO ACHIEVE THE BUDGET

Earlier in this book, in the chapter "Change drivers in budgeting", I explained the importance of using change drivers in corporate budgeting. In the company's previous financial year, all the change drivers that were monitored represent the tools needed to achieve the change objectives in the company's budget. The company's budgeting process should select the most appropriate change drivers and use them to determine which change drivers will be used to achieve the target budget outputs for the company during the budget period. In practice, this means that for each change driver selected, an objective, in practice a change target, must be defined. The change targets for the change drivers together form the operational change target for the whole company, the achievement of which is a prerequisite for the company to achieve the budgeted targets.

A company's budget figures always include the need for changes in the company's operations. The use of change drivers makes the objectives of the company's performance changes and the planning and monitoring of the measures required to achieve them more concrete. Once the change drivers and their objectives have been selected to achieve the company's budget objectives, the next step is to define the measures that will be taken to achieve these objectives in the company. In the change management methodology, the CHANGE DRIVER tool for this purpose is the development of action plans. In all three of the books I have written in the past – "KOKO YRITYKSEN KAPASITEETTI TEHOKÄYT-TÖÖN", "YRITYKSEN VOIMAVARAT HYÖTYKÄYTTÖÖN – YHTEIS-VOIMIN" and "RESURSSIEN TULOKSILLA YRITYKSEN TAVOITE-TULOKSEEN" – I have presented a model for drawing up action plans and explained in detail how to draw them up and how to monitor the results achieved. For this reason, I will not repeat these points here.

I would like to take this opportunity to highlight a few important issues related to the use of action plans in the context of corporate budgeting.

1. The first important point is to be aware of the need for change in the company's profit and loss figures contained in the company budget, i.e. the target change in terms of profit and loss figures.

2. The second important thing is to know how each of the possible change drivers available to the company can affect the company's profit and loss figures.

3. The third important thing is to choose the right change drivers and the change targets for them, for example, the change driver represented by the need to change the utilisation rate from 85% to 90%.

4. The fourth important thing is to appoint the person responsible for the change.

5. The fifth important thing is to identify concrete measures to achieve the change and schedule their implementation.

6. Sixth, monitor the achievement of the objectives and, if negative deviations occur, plan and implement corrective measures to achieve the objectives.

Identifying and applying change drivers is an ongoing learning process in the company. Here is how I have applied this continuous learning process both to myself and to others in companies. The continuous learning process should start by stopping and answering the following questions, for example, at the end of each working week:

1. What were your objectives for the week just ended:

    1.1 How many hours of my working week were to be spent on tasks that would improve the company's performance?

    1.2 How many hours of my working week were to be spent on tasks that did not affect the company's performance?

    1.3 How many hours of my working week did I spend on tasks that improved the company's performance?

    1.4 How many hours of my working week did I spend on tasks that did not affect the company's performance?

2. What will I use in the next working week to better achieve my objectives in the next working week?

    2.1   Which tasks can I leave undone in the future because they do not affect the company's performance?

    2.2   Which tasks will I increase in the next working week, and how much will they represent of my working hours in the following week, so that by doing them I will achieve my objectives better in the following week than in the previous week?

These questions should be answered concretely and honestly. It is usually the case that more than half of the working hours in a working week are spent on tasks other than improving the company's performance. Once this has been established, the respondent usually starts to explain to himself or herself what prevented him or her from carrying out more tasks related to improving the company's performance. Another typical explanation is that, for almost all of their activities and the hours spent on them, the respondent convinces themselves that yes, they are related to improving the company's performance, but the impact is not immediately visible in the company's performance. When this happened to me, I realised that I was only deceiving myself with these answers. It is better to face the truth and believe in the results of my own monitoring. They don't lie. If I continue to lie to myself and distort my own actions and their results, I am committing self-deception. This is where I start to think differently about what has happened. It's really great that I realised myself, before my boss, how much of my working time I was spending on anything other than improving the company's performance. I told myself that the truth was reflected in my track record, which I started keeping track of. As I continued this continuous learning process for a few weeks, I weeded out the unnecessary work and the percentage of my working week spent on improving the company's performance increased by tens of percent. Once I achieved my goal of using weekly working time appropriately, I then moved on to the next stage in the continuous learning process, which was to improve the efficiency of the work I was doing. This was done by making a weekly record: How much of my working week was spent doing things to improve the company's performance? What tasks did I do? And what results did I achieve? Once I had this tracking in place, I focused my weekly analysis on: How did I do my tasks and how could I do them differently to achieve better results?

When you work in this way, my experience is that the effectiveness of achieving results in your own work is multiplied many times over. The root cause of the improvement in results achieved by using this continuous learning process is, in my opinion, the development of my own powers of observation and right way of thinking. I encourage everyone to try this continuous learning process and enjoy the results! This joy of discovery should not be left here, but should be shared with colleagues. Why should not others also be encouraged to try this continuous learning process?

QUOTE CALCULATION

Quotation typically relates to project business, i.e. an activity where a set of defined services is offered at a fixed price, within defined limits and under defined conditions. What is too often overlooked in these situations is the boundaries of service delivery. This typically results in the buyer's perception of the transaction being that unforeseen circumstances during the project will not impose additional costs on the buyer, even if they are attributable to the buyer. The supplier's perception of the transaction is typically that any additional costs arising from unexpected change situations can be charged to the buyer by the supplier in addition to the fixed cap price. The worse the buyer has planned and defined the content of the project delivery it has purchased, the more problematic the supplier's ability to price its bid correctly, resulting in a larger dispute.

When it comes to the project business, I recommend that companies include tender calculations in their performance monitoring. This can be done in two ways:

1. Tracking the content of the bid invoice for the first bid against the content of the bid invoice used by the company to place the order for the bid. In addition, the actual cost of the project is monitored against the order's quotation, i.e. the actual profitability of the order received compared to the company's budgeting requirements for the actual profitability of the project.

2. Monitoring the extent to which the realised costs of the project corresponded to the order quotation, i.e. the realised profitability of the order received compared to the level of realised profitability of the project as defined in the company's budgeting.

Of the above options, the latter is easier to implement. The purpose of the first performance monitoring is:

1. To teach tender calculators to calculate more accurately the tender prices in relation to the costs actually incurred.

2. To encourage bid calculators to discuss with project production why the actual project costs differ from the prices in the bid calculations, i.e. the bid calculators learn better what project production is capable of, and project production learns how to better implement the costs of the bids submitted in the future.

3. To teach the company's project vendors how to negotiate in the right way, so that in the future the variance between the initial bid on a project and the bid that led to the buyer's order is reduced.

VARIANCES BETWEEN BUDGET AND ACTUAL FIGURES

Financial management of a company using change drivers

The CHANGE DRIVER change management method makes it possible to obtain information on the deviations from the achievement of the company's budget targets and their root causes throughout the company organisation for each person in the company, i.e. how well they have been able to achieve their targets. Deviations can be as follows:

1. Either the variances are positive, meaning that the company's budget targets have been achieved better than budgeted. Of course, it is important to be satisfied with the fact that the budget targets have been exceeded and to give positive feedback to the company's staff, both in general and, in particular, at individual level, in as concrete a way as possible. This is also an excellent opportunity for the company to raise enthusiasm for delivering results. At the same time, it is worthwhile to collect the experience of exceeding budget targets, i.e. the answers to the questions: what are the reasons why this has happened and who has made it possible, so that personal feedback can be given.

2. Or the variances are negative, which means that the company's budget objectives have not been met.

The deviations in the achievement of the company's budget objectives show that the change measures planned in the company's budgeting process to achieve the company's budget objectives have not had the intended impact on the company's actual results. The financial management of a company using change drivers – the CHANGE DRIVER change management method – makes it possible to identify the deviations in the figures showing realisation of the company's budget objectives on the basis of the following reports/monitoring:

1. The company's operational profit and loss account report.

2. The company's profitability monitoring reports by accounting object.

3. The monitoring of the implementation of the change drivers and the related action plans for the selected change targets in the company:

   3.1 By change target in the company.

   3.2 By accounting target.

   3.3 By core business processes.

   3.4 By phase of core business processes.

   3.5 By resource (by person and by machine).

With these variance monitors, the company can identify the concrete root causes of any performance deviations and quickly start planning and implementing corrective measures for negative performance deviations. The sooner a company takes action, the sooner negative deviations can be corrected, thus minimising the potential problems caused by negative deviations.

FORECASTING

In my second book, "YRITYKSEN VOIMAVARAT HYÖTYKÄYT-TÖÖN – YHETSIVOIMIN", I talked about predicting your company's performance. Here are some more of my experiences. Depending on the company's business, the company's profit forecasts can be based on, among other things, the following data:

1. The company's order book data, especially for product manufacturing and project-based business.

2. Information from the company's customers, where the company's business is based on long-term and in-depth cooperation with customers.

3. The company's quotation database.

4. Information on ongoing contract negotiations and their status assessments.

5. The data on the actual outturn figures at the beginning of the budget period compared with the data on the objectives at the beginning of the budget period and the estimates based on these data.

6. The data on the results achieved at the beginning of the budget period compared with the data on the results achieved in the previous budget period and the estimates based on these data.

7. Data based solely on subjective feelings.

8. Information on market trends.

Based on my experience, the above list is in order of importance. This means that a company's order book data is the most reliable source of information for making business performance forecasts.

The use of market trend information to forecast a company's business performance is the most unreliable, especially when the impact of market trends on company performance is predicted by someone other than the company itself. This is because there is no third party that can use general market research to gather reliable information from the market that a company can use with confidence to forecast its performance. No two companies in the market are alike, and therefore performance forecasts must be based on company-specific information. Of course, market research can be carried out either by the company itself or by an external party. It should be borne in mind that the better the company knows the business needs and situations of its customers, and the more open the exchange of information between the company and its customers, the better the company can use the information it receives from its customers to forecast its own business performance.

Management

In this book, business management is economic management, based on the CHANGE DRIVER method of change management, using change drivers. This management is a continuous process. This continuous process, from the point of view of the front-line manager, consists of the following steps:

1. Collect data from the follow-ups.

2. Set performance targets for the employee.

3. Use change drivers to implement the performance targets.

4. Develop an action plan with actions that the employee must take to achieve the performance targets. Whenever possible, involve the employee in developing the action plan.

5. Monitor the achievement of the employee's performance targets and provide feedback to the employee on the achievement of the performance targets.

6. Draw up a corrective action plan with the employee, which the employee must implement if the employee's performance targets are not met.

7. Monitor the corrective actions taken by the employee to see if they lead to the achievement of the performance targets, and provide feedback to the employee on the achievement

of the performance targets. If the employee's performance targets are not met, return to step 6.

8. When the employee is able to achieve his/her performance targets, give the employee feedback. Depending on the workplace practices, reward the employee according to any performance bonus and engagement rules that the company may have in place.

This ongoing process is an excellent way for the manager to communicate the company's financial principles to the employee and to get the employee to work in a way that achieves the related objectives, so that the employee learns and is inspired to produce information about his/her work and activities that the manager can use to develop the company's business. Here are a few tips for doing this:

1. Teach the employee to recognise which steps in the work process are unnecessary and tell the employee how their possible elimination will affect the employee's results.

2. Teach the employee to identify those steps in the work process that customers do not want to pay for. The employee should be told how their possible elimination will affect the employee's ability to achieve results. Customers are willing to pay for added value from the supplier. They do not want to pay for unnecessary activities in the supplier's production, like transfers and walks.

3. Encourage employees to think about how to simplify and speed up their work. The employee should be told how simplifying and speeding up the way he or she does his or her work will affect the results he or she achieves.

Rewarding and engaging

In my opinion, there are two aspects to the engagement of a company's employees in the company's financial business, depending on the duration of the engagement, which are:

1. The short-term perspective, which motivates people with financial incentives to perform at their best in the short term.

2. The long-term perspective, which uses financial incentives to motivate people to engage and deliver the best possible performance in the long term.

In my first book, "KOKO YRITYKSEN KAPASITEETTI TEHO-KÄYTTÖÖN", I talked about motivating and engaging people in the company, so I won't repeat that here. In this context, I want to highlight the different options for engaging a company's employees, namely financial engagement. It is above all a question of the means by which it is possible and desirable to encourage company staff to achieve the best possible results for the company on an ongoing basis – always staying in line with the defined objectives.

The first question for the company is how each person can influence the company's performance through his or her own actions and what is his or her motivation, in terms of financial incentive, to give his or her all to the company's performance. The solution presented in this book to the question of how change drivers can create the conditions for the financial management of the firm, using the CHANGE DRIVER change management method, provides answers to this question. Change drivers are concrete performance measures for each person in the company to see concretely the impact of his or her actions and actions, and their development, on the company's performance. When a person has the will to become involved in the financial management of the company through change drivers, opportunities open up for him or her to make a direct and indirect impact on the company's performance.

For the company, another question is how much the company's financial incentives can increase the willingness, drive and motivation of individuals to improve their contribution to the company's performance. The answer to this question depends on the company, its situation and each person's own interest in achieving the financial benefits and other incentives offered by the company. It depends, of course, on each individual himself, so the answer to this question can only be found by asking the company's staff.

The financial incentives I presented in my first book, "KOKO YRITYKSEN KAPASITEETTI TEHOKÄYTTÖÖN", provide solutions for financially encouraging each person in the company to work and develop within the company and "to give their best", either in the short or long term. Short-term financial incentives are typically performance bonuses paid to individuals by the company. Long-term financial incentives are not only about encouraging a person to work hard, but also about engaging them to do their best for the company. Long-term financial incentives include: a directed share issue, a transaction between the company, i.e. the owners of the company and the employee, with or without subscription or purchase price for debt, and options.

STEPS TO IMPLEMENTING THE CHANGE DRIVERS FOR CORPORATE FINANCIAL MANAGEMENT

With the change drivers of corporate financial management, it is advisable to implement the change in stages. I recommend a phased implementation as follows:

1. Ensure that your company has the right electronic information systems in place, that they have sufficient features, in particular a sufficient number of accounting objects to deploy, and that a sufficient number of accounting objects can be included in the accounting object cursor. If your company does not have an electronic BI system in place and your company's electronic financial management system does not have adequate reporting capabilities, find out what type of electronic BI system is best suited to your company's needs.

2. Make sure that the company's accounting is done in the right way, e.g. that accounting entries, accruals, reconciliations and provisions are done correctly, and that clear written instructions on how to do this are in place and in use. It is also worth ensuring that the company has adequate accounting skills (either as an in-house service or as a purchased service).

3. Define for the company the content of the accounting objects and the accounting object identifier cursor. Ensure that they are available in all of the company's electronic operational systems.

4. Define the content of the operational profit and loss account for the company and ensure that it is available in the company's electronic financial management system for budgeting and performance reporting.

5. Define the content of the company's accounting reports.

6. Implement the profitability monitoring of the accounting objects in the correct sequence and in a step-by-step manner. The order of implementation should take into account the business and its situation.

7. Determine the monitoring needs related to the change drivers at the level of the company and its functions and start the monitoring. Once sufficient monitoring data is available, introduce the selected change drivers at the level of the company and its functions into management for budgeting and then for budget execution monitoring.

8. Initiate customer meetings between the company's functions and their customers to agree on services, their contents, operational rules and objectives.

9. Define the stages of the core processes for the company's activities, what is done at each stage and what the stages produce.

10. Where appropriate, define the monitoring needs for the change drivers by phase of the activities and start monitoring them. Once sufficient monitoring data is available, use the selected change drivers at the stage level of the company's activities for management purposes in budgeting and then for budget execution monitoring.

11. Systematically and continuously maintain and develop the use of change drivers in the financial management of the company's capacity and resources.

Outcome

In this book, I have focused in particular on providing answers to the following questions:

What types of financial problems do businesses typically face?

What are the main types of financial problems encountered by businesses?

What are the main types of financial problems that firms face?

What means are available in companies to remedy the shortcomings in the conditions for financial management in companies?

How should corporate financial management be put into practice in order to enable companies to achieve their financial objectives on a continuous basis?

The answers to all these questions involve understanding the purpose of change drivers, realising their potential uses and being able to apply them to specific cases. I would like to reiterate here that the use of change drivers must be learned, and they need to be applied individually, depending on the company and its situation.

Change drivers are performance measures used in a company to measure the impact of changes in activities on the company's performance.

Before the relevant and sufficiently comprehensive set of change drivers needed to change the firm's performance can be identified, the firm's management must have access to sufficiently detailed financial monitoring and relevant efficiency monitoring of the firm's operations. Based on the potential for change in the results of these monitoring exercises and their impact on performance, the change drivers for the company and the associated targets, as well as the necessary measures for the responsible persons to achieve the performance targets, will be defined.

It is very important to find only the essential drivers of change in the company's activities and to focus on the implementation of the related objectives. It is not worth monitoring everything in the company or defining change drivers for every aspect, as unnecessary monitoring will lead to unnecessary costs. The important thing is to focus on concrete, measurable opportunities when selecting change drivers. If, for example, the company later needs to increase its monitoring of operational efficiency in order to identify the associated opportunities for change and their effects, the use of change drivers can always be expanded. If a company introduces change drivers that either are not essential to changing the company, or else prove not to have the desired tangible impact on the company's performance, then the company's staff may well become frustrated and start to see the use of change drivers as a tiresome obligation. When you start with change drivers that can be used to achieve the desired changes in performance figures as easily and quickly as possible, the staff will become enthusiastic about using them and will want to find more change drivers in order to achieve further positive results. My motto on this issue is:

"Successes increase the willingness to change and failures reduce the willingness to change. If you always have the right attitude, the motivation to change never disappears."

The use of change drivers should be started with the help of someone who has experience in using them, so that you learn how to apply them in the right way. It is only through experimentation and concrete practical experience and results that you will then become the best practitioner of change drivers in business change situations.

When a company has put in place the conditions for financial management in the way I have described in this book, and operates according to the FLOW concept and the CHANGE DRIVER method of change management that I have presented in my previous books, then the company has the conditions to achieve its performance targets on a continuous basis. In addition, the company will then have its resources at its disposal and the entire capacity of the company will be at its most efficient at all times. The better a company learns to understand how changes can have a concrete impact on its performance, and the better all people in the company understand how their actions can contribute to the company's performance, the better the results the company will be able to achieve. It is worth bearing in mind that, even if the company's performance objectives do not change, achieving each of the company's budget targets will require changes in the way the company operates, because the business environment is constantly changing. In other words, change is a necessity for a company to continue to operate and therefore change is an ongoing process within a company. If you are open, curious and enthusiastic about change, you will be able to see it as an opportunity and not as an obstacle.

From all four of these books, it's worth remembering the following principle I learned from my orienteering experience, which applies equally to change management:

Know exactly where you are on the map. Know exactly where you need to go next on the map, i.e. where the next tick is. Identify on the map all the options on how to proceed to the next tick. Since time is the most important measure of performance in orienteering, choose the route that will take you to the next checkpoint the fastest. As you proceed along your chosen route, make sure that you can read the terrain well enough to know where you are going on the map throughout your progress to the next checkpoint, otherwise you will be lost. The end result will then only depend on your fitness. The better you have developed your map-reading skills before orienteering and the better your fitness, the faster you will be able to move from one obstacle to the next. In this context, the progression from track to track represents the need for change and the navigator is the agent of change. The route you choose represents a plan to progress to the goal, i.e. the next obstacle. The course director of the entire navigation event has set a target time for each of the checkpoints, i.e. what the course director's ideal time is for moving from one checkpoint to the next.

Finally, to summarise my thoughts on the matter:

"Challenges make life interesting. Uncompromising will, doing and constantly finding a better way of doing things are the means to achieve your goals. Anything is possible."

Sources

Alhola, K. 2016. Toimintolaskenta. 5. uudistettu painos. Helsinki: Alma Talent Oy.

Alma. 2024. Netti: https://www.almatalent.fi/tunnuslukuopas/kannattavuus/oman-paaoman-tuotto-prosentti-roe/. Alma Talent Oy.

Carder, S. 2020. Power your profits. Atria paperback.

Fiber, B. 1995. Double your profit in 6 months or less, HarperBusiness.

Grasso, L. 2005.

Harvard Business Review (HBR'S 10 MUST READS), 2023. On Performance Management.

Harvard Business Review, 2017. HBR Guide to Performance Management.

Ikäheimo, S., Malmi, T. & Walden, R. 2016. Yrityksen laskentatoimi. Alma Talent Oy. Ekirja [viitattu 28.9.2019]. Saatavissa: https://verkkokirjahylly-almatalent-fi.aineistot.lamk.fi/teos/JADBHXGUG#kohta:Yrityksen((20) laskentatoimi((20)(:Johdanto((20)(:Laskentatoimen((20) osaalueet((20)/piste:b487.

Järvenpää, M., Länsiluoto, A., Partanen, V. & Pellinen, J. 2010. Talousohjaus ja kustannuslaskenta. Helsinki: WSOYpro Oy.

Kaplan, R. & Anderson, S. 2004.

Kirjanpitolaki. 30.12.1997/1336 muutoksineen, joista viimeisin 1249/2023.

Manninen, J., Yrityksen koko kapasiteetti tehokäyttöön, 2022, Books on Demand (BoD).

Manninen, J., Yrityksen voimavarat hyötykäyttöön – yhteisvoimin, 2023, Books on Demand (BoD).

Manninen, J., Resurssien tuloksilla yrityksen tavoitetulokseen, 2023, Books on Demand (BoD).

Marr, B.2012. Key Performance Indicators. FT publishing.

Osakeyhtiölaki 624, 2006.

Pellinen, J. 2019. Kustannuslaskenta ja kannattavuusajattelu. 3. uudistettu painos. Helsinki: Alma Talent Oy.

Raudasoja, K. & Johansson, M.–L. 2009. Esimies talouden johtajana julkishallinnossa. Alma Talent Oy. E-kirja [viitattu 28.9.2019]. Saatavissa: https://verkkokirjahylly-almatalent-fi.aineistot.lamk.fi/teos/DABBXXBTAFDCH#/historiaan: https(:(/(/verkkokirjahylly-almatalent-fi.aineistot.lamk.fi(/ etusivu(23)Uusimmat(/haku(:toimintolaskenta/kohta:1.

Siegele, J. 2014.

Tilastot, 2024. Kaupparekisteri.

Tilastot, 2024. Patentti- ja rekisterihallitus.

Tilastot, 2024. Suomen Asiakastieto Oy.

Toivanen, T. https://www.ttvalmennus.fi/post/ mit%C3%A4tarkoittaa-hyv%C3%A4-kirjanpitotapa, 2020.

Turney, P. 2002. Toimintolaskenta – Avain tuottavampaan toimintaan. 2. uudistettu painos. Helsinki: Tietosanoma Oy.

About me

I am Jarmo Manninen, engineer, MHT, BPS, MBA. I have a very broad and diverse education and practical experience in the business development of small and medium-sized enterprises (SMEs) as a manager, consultant and trainer in Finland and abroad.

I started my career in corporate management at the Uusikaupunki car factory, working for the predecessor of the current Valmet Automotive Oy, Oy Saab-Valmet Ab, first as Maintenance Manager and then as Automation Manager. Since then, I have been Managing Director of 30 manufacturing and service companies in Finland, Malaysia, Singapore, Russia and Ukraine, responsible for planning and implementing the changes needed to achieve the objectives of these companies.

I have been the director of two national projects in Finland. The first was a business restructuring project. My responsibility was to develop a solution for how M&A could help companies to achieve their defined objectives, which in 70% of M&A cases had never been achieved before. Then I was responsible for training consultants to implement the solution in different parts of Finland. My second national project was a project to improve the profitability of companies. My responsibility was to develop a solution whereby business advisers and consultants could help companies change their operations so that they achieve their targets on an ongoing basis, especially in terms of profitability. I was then responsible for training business advisers and consultants in different areas who would put the solution into practice in companies.

As a consultant, I have helped over 300 companies in the retail, manufacturing and service industries to improve their business to achieve their goals. As a consultant I have worked in companies and have also run business clinics in Helsinki, Espoo, Vantaa and Tampere. These business clinics became very popular due to the results they achieved, where my promise was to find a solution for entrepreneurs to any problem in achieving their goals in a one and a half hour meeting.

I have developed a change management method for companies called the CHANGE DRIVER. This method enables companies to leverage the full capacity of the company, to harness the company's resources through a collective effort and to use the resources to achieve the company's target results. I have written four books on the CHANGE DRIVER and its application in practice, of which this book is the fourth in this series.

I currently work part time. For more information about my background, please see my LinkedIn profile: https://www.linkedin.com/in/jarmo-manninen-a9b295b/.